T0197249

SAVING AMERICA

SAVING AMERICA

BILLY WILSON

 iUniverse

SAVING AMERICA

iUniverse books may be ordered through booksellers or by contacting:

iUniverse
1663 Liberty Drive
Bloomington, IN 47403
www.iuniverse.com
1-800-Authors (1-800-288-4677)

ISBN: 978-1-5320-5140-1 (sc)
ISBN: 978-1-5320-5141-8 (e)

Library of Congress Control Number: 2018906724

Print information available on the last page.

iUniverse rev. date: 06/06/2018

1

"EDUCATION"

THIS COUNTRY WAS CHRISTENED in the name of the Lord Jesus Christ. Our Supreme Court has ruled and confirmed twice that this is a Christian nation. Obama announced to the world, it was not a Christian nation anymore. I am sure he had dreams of turning it into a Muslim Nation, he said so and just about did. Obama is a Muslim and obviously and plainly the biggest liar that has ever gotten into American Politics until this day.

There are two words that best cover the legal papers of this country. The Bible and our Constitution, they should never be allowed to be changed or monkeyed with without proper authority, and that means from up-above or the Bible, God's Word. They are what this country was built upon, its very foundation. We have a Christian Constitution, and a Christian Declaration of Independence. Muslim faith will not fit under either one of them, not in the stretch of their imagination. The Bible and God will never be changed, neither will our Constitution if we keep and believe in them.

To change either one would mean to change our country and deny our Christian faith. This is exactly what the "Mark of the Beast" is, an oath to do just that. I do not believe our country will every need changing. It is built upon God's Holy Word and he says his Word will never change.

The Constitution protects the Bible; the Bible protects the Constitution, neither one can be changed, and this country survive. They must both be protected from the God hating, liberal, Devil-possessed, politicians that are working overtime to destroy them both. The Democrats have been trying to divide and crush this country ever since they lost the Civil War, and before. That was what all our wars were about. Democrats are just like the Devil, they don't ever give up, divide and conquer.

Man is About constantly changing, and I agree he probably needs to, but he is never to be removed from the boundaries of God's Word. God has given man no conditions to do such a thing. Do you know another country that has "One nation under God" in its pledge to their flag? This is the reason all God hating atheist hates this country and all of God's people in it? They have demanded all us people that know God to remove it from our pledge and made it unlawful for us to say it? What can be their reasoning for desiring such a thing? What can be our reasoning for allowing them to? People that don't know God cannot seem to recognize his enemies. I believe our forefathers, that built this country and fought and died to keep it, would get sick and throw up to see God's so-called people that are running it today. Makes me think God may feel the same way.

I am not advocating an armed rebellion against our government. But if that is what it takes to prevent our government from taking away our freedom to <u>worship as one pleases.</u> Then I am ready to pick up my arms to go with the people the very reason we pulled out of England and Europe. Now they are trying to force their religion upon us. If one does not study history, he will repeat it over again. Our forefathers fought the world, and many died for that right for us. Our adversaries, Mystery Babylon Democrats, are pushing hard for another Civil War in this country, the same ones that started the first one, they need to be watched-out for, to keep this nation from being tore completely down this time.

Every hear the saying, divide and conquer? It is the very moto of Satan himself. I do not know if he originated it or just picked it up. He sure has made a tool of it. Started our Civil war with it and trying for another. If God's people would just unite under the Word of God, Satan wouldn't have a prayer to get one started with.

The most valuable thing that one generation can give to the next generation, that it is bringing on, is Knowledge of God's Word. And a knowledge of how and what our country was built upon. God is a Spirit, so his knowledge must be a spiritual word and knowledge. I am sure that is not a real familiar word to the young children of today, but it was not a strange thing to me when my momma used to read to me the Bible seventy-five years ago. I was too young to understand all the words, but I can still feel that same Spirit today when I read my Bible. If you can explain that to me, then I can explain to you, when you ask me what I am talking about.

A Spiritual knowledge and education is all made up with Spiritual Words from the Bible. If a word is not found in the King James Authorized Bible, that Jesus himself said he wrote, how can it be a spiritual word? It is the only writing in this world, wrote by the Spirit of God, saying it is not to be changed or substituted in any way. Any other word, English or not, is a carnal word and making up a carnal education and must be excepted as such.

God may not keep on protecting and building this country, but he will keep on protecting and backing his Word and anybody that believes in it. God's Word does not use the word *education* in it, making it a carnal word. Carnal words cannot be accepted to pay a spiritual debt, neither can a spiritual word pay or explain a carnal debt.

Let us try a few examples; will a bank or a church, cash a check wrote on God or the Spirit of God?

Would you? Even if you are a good Christian? Suppose the company you are working for tells you they are going to start paying you in spiritual money; you are a Christian and God is going to give it to you in dollars. Are you going to tell him you cannot trust your God, or maybe God does not have the money? Most people are completely carnal and blind and cannot recognize spiritual money and think they have no use for it. God says, he owns all the money of the world. What is the paymaster supposed to believe? What do you believe? Carnal is carnal and spiritual is spiritual. This book is written for nothing but the Spiritual side of man.

The both of you should know that carnal and spiritual has no equal values, they will not mix in anything when it comes to values or comparisons in any way. It is difficult for common man to conceive he is living in two different worlds at the same time. Do you think when God made this creation six-thousand years ago, that it was the beginning of God and his only world? That person needs to pray threw.

Let us say the bank teller gave you the money because he knows that God is faithful. Who will make the money up to the banks-head at the end of the day when the teller turns his money in? Somebody will have to fill the hole with a signature and pay the money or someone will be fired, if not jailed. The Carnal can only pay the carnal debt, the spirit can only pay the debt for the spiritual. Neither one can pay a debt for the other. Any word can be a carnal word but only a word found in or established in the Bible can be a spiritual word.

This would eliminate a lot of confusion if it could be fully received and understood. Very few people seem to know that the carnal and spiritual are two different worlds. They try to judge one by the other. There is no way to compare the two and everybody is thinking one way or the other. To play both sides of a word for one's benefit is what God calls a _double minded person_, says he is unstable in all his ways. To operate as a Christian, one must recognize which one he is dealing with and dealing from. Can one be a Christian and not know the Spirit of God? If it was me and I was not sure; I would be trying to learn the Spirit of God.

Most Christians seem to think God has said for us to not deal evenly with a person without the Spirit of God, and we should be able to know the man. When God said, not to be unequally yoked with an unbeliever, you can know he was using Spiritual Words. If one has the spirit or not. What God said was; "We are not to judge the man, but the Spirit. If we cannot be around the lost, we would have to get out of the world." We are to treat a spirit by the way the spirit is reacting to Truth.

How has he told us to treat a person that is lost in the wrong spirit? That should give one something to study his Bible about, all of it, if one wants to be a Christian. One cannot treat all men alike for there are no two of them just alike. But the Spirit of God must be treated like the Spirit, for it will never change, not even from person to person. The carnal should be recognized, and one must treat it for what it is, it goes with the person, but must die out to the Spirit of God.

Truth is Christ and will never be wrong. The other man may not be any more lost than the first, if they are dealing in truth the Bible will lead them in the truth if they will learn how to read it and agree. The Bible is Truth. Then they can both help each other and show others the right way and have Jesus Christ to help them. He is the K. J. Bible, he is the Truth in all the world.

The word *education* is not found in the Bible, or the Constitution. It is a carnal word and has no spiritual meaning of its own. The Bible recognizes the carnal words by their Spiritual meaning and from the way they are used. I did not find the word education in our Declaration of Independence either. The Bible does not mention it for the very contents of the Bible itself is Truth, so is the other documents mentioned in this paragraph, they are all truth, making them all spiritual papers, and have stood for a record time. The constitution protects the Bible and the Bible protects our Constitution. If God hating hypocrites are not allowed to change them they will stand for more record time. The Bible does not have one excess word in it and does not have a necessary-word left out of it. Ever wonder why Jesus said? "He did not want man messing around with what he wrote in the Bible." If man changes one thing in it, it will not be God's Word anymore. Now, you know why he said it. Every word in the King James Bible is a Spiritual Word.

Jesus told men to establish each word with no less than two or three witnesses from God's Word then it can be called a Gospel Word. Said so in six places I found in my Bible. If God's People would receive and practice that, there would not be *but* one denomination in the world. It would be the established Word of God by the Word of God, just like the Bible. Do not squawk to me about other languages, Jesus wrote his word in the English Language because England sought him for it at a desperate time. King James Authorized it, and it went almost instantly into the leading language of the world.

Jesus said he wrote it and blessed it. They received it joyfully in around sixteen-hundred A D. It saved England from the "Mother of all Harlots and Abominations of the World Church" until they went to government there at Rome for a God. They have been falling off God's map ever since. After England, America received it, and separated from all of Europe. It is the only thing that will save anybody from the Whore at Rome, then, now, or in the end. Read about it from your Bible there in Revelations. God has told us all things, if we know God we will believe him.

It will cost one his life after he has taken the Mark of the Beast, for he has sworn allegiance and his very being, to a false god. I have a book being published called the "Mark of the Beast." You will be able to purchase it anywhere books are sold. Yes, education is a very broad word, used and worshiped much by the carnal world but has no identity indication about it to the spiritual. The world likes it, because it keeps them from needing to use "God's Word," which they hate and want to take from our language. Our founding fathers were required to memorize chapters in the Bible to acquire their college diploma. Our colleges have come a long way, just look at them, they have lost their compass and do not know where they are going.

This country was very well built upon meals in the homes being prepared at certain times and on time. George Washington said, "No man could rightly rule on this earth without the Bible." He always prayed and thanked God for all the meals in his home. He always, in his home, said the blessing himself unless there was a minister present. The minister would say the blessing. He always acknowledged God in everything he did. The Indians he fought, highly believed he was a Spirit-sent soldier, that could not be killed. American History well backs them up, if we could teach it to our kids.

Babylon will not allow us to do that. One Indian testified that he pulled his rifle down on Washington, point blank, no less than four times in one battle but he came out unhurt, but his army reported after one battle, four bullet holes were found in his coat. Not one of my three children I raised went one day to a government school but they all finished the twelfth grade. And went on to attain several degrees in colleges of their choice. That made my job as their preacher, twice as difficult.

You can tell these God hating, hypocritical, atheist, Mystery Babylon, trying to destroy this nation today, that this government was founded completely upon the Word of Jesus Christ. Our founding fathers would have died before allowing it any other way. Many of them did die. If we Christians would just stand up in that fact, it would be as dangerous as a little kid playing in the fireplace for anyone to mess with us. We have allowed this country to sink so low in the filth of this world that I am sure we would now have to prove ourselves to God, before he would pick us up and build us up again. The first thing he asks from any man is repentance, he asks that from every man. It comes from one's heart. God knows the thoughts and intents of every heart and looks nowhere else for it.

The carnal word, *education,* is as worthless to God as a sidesaddle on a hog. He never used the word in any of his writings. Mystery Babylon at Rome, that has now completely gained control of our entire school system and everything else, from Washing D C, down to head start. Has told us, right to our face, that Christ and God's Word will not be tolerated anywhere around our own Government properties, and certainly not our children, to them they are government property. And we are wondering around in the darkness as to what happened and who it is that is trying to divide us up and completely conquer us. I often say, if Obama knew two people he would be trying to divide them. How blind can one people get? What will it take to wake them up? One would think there is enough in what I just wrote to wake up the dead.

The Democrats have spent our money well into the time of our great grandchildren. With plenty of help from the Republicans. Telling us that it is pleasing to our God and he will bless us for it. Politicians, being this country's Christians worst enemy on the planet.

Can you believe, with the liberal politicians we have, the money we owe will ever be paid back?

The Republicans are too weak-kneed to hold up a grown man. Neither side knows a thing about God. God said, in the second chapter of the Book to the Romans, that the man that is *accusing* another, is guilty of the same thing. One of the more amazing scriptures I have read. I questioned and tested that for years before I could completely believe it fully, I have never found it to be wrong yet. It is best seen and checked, in politics. It sticks out to me now like a hand with two sore thumbs that it is so.

The reason it sounds so weak and a little bit fuzzy is, I cannot find it backed up two places in the Bible, to establish the clear way, *accuse*, is meant. It cannot be sworn to mean, that because a man has made a statement, *it* is what is making him guilty of the same thing, for there is a question between stating the truth or just accusing someone. I do not believe that stating the truth can fully be called accusing. If he is accusing someone when he does not know the truth of the matter, he is basically guilty for he has a guilty heart and mind for sure, and you can bet on it. To that extent, I have never seen it fail. Use that statement on our politicians today. I believe you might be amazed. You might be able to see a little about why I detest Democrats and about all other politicians.

Mystery Babylon Democrat Schools are teaching in all our schools and on the TV, that it is the Republicans that are always wrong, and have taken all the money away from the poor people, and the ones that have us twenty trillion dollars in debt. I see that as accusing and they are certainly guilty of lying. They could not sell that *sermon* to one Christian that knows and has read his Bible or true American history. Yet, Mystery Babylon has sold it to our whole country, and the country has sold it to the children, it is plainly a lie. Why do you think they are demanding that our Bible and Constitution must be buried? It tells us to kill them before allowing them to take the place of our God, and that is where they think they are already at, setting in his seat. God will bless any government or people, if they will fear and respect him, and allow the Lord to be their God. If you are a Christian you will not lie, and God says you are not to believe a lie. That alone would clean up our country.

We have preachers telling us that God has laid it on *his* people to meet all the needs of the world, which is a complete lie. So, they start in on us to have a heart for the children. I *do* have a heart for children, but I cannot feed enough of the kids of the world to hardly effect one child. I do not see the Democrats feeding them anything but lies and promises and things that do not belong to them and just enough in the right places to get the votes. The kids will starve to death if they depend on the Liberal Democrats to feed them. I see not one spot in my Bible where God told me that was my job or responsibility, other than my own children. God has not told his people they are to feed the ungodly people of the world nor their children. I have not learned to love or believe lying preachers, are any preachers that think they are setting in God's seat. God has said, only his Word will set there, and preachers are called to teach his Word. My God says he hates every liar. Maybe we should send a few of them up to God, see if they might preach to him. Maybe they could get him converted. They are not very productive down here.

We attained the Idea of taking our kids out of our homes and letting somebody else teach and feed them, from the Mystery Babylon Whore there at Rome that simply believe they are God. We spend *trillions* of taxpayer's dollars building useless carnal crap in the pretense it is making our kids smart and safe. Sending busses over the world ever day to take the children from the homes as far away from their parents and families as they can get away with. So, Mystery Babylon can teach them in their ways, and the children belong to them. When it is common sense that the more money and effort we put into it, the more problems and less true learning the kids get. I have worked much time on this, the best I can come up with is they reach maybe ten per-cent of the children, the rest of them are spinning in the wind somewhere. But we have given all them to Babylon for nothing in return.

Trying to teach all kids in one bunch, teach them all the same things, telling them what they are to do and become, teach them *everything*, no regard to what one is qualified to do or interested in doing. God has told us nowhere, to raise our children in any such way. But has told us the opposite. A kid raised in a home in a familiar and loving environment would at least have an even chance, even the ten per-cent that they reach very well might learn to provide for and keep a home and raise a family. They sure do not learn it now with Mystery Babylon sitting in their face.

They could pass all the reasonable laws the people wanted, like every child that is capable should learn to read and write and some about numbers, before he becomes of age. Parents that are just too sorry to give their kids a chance, by teaching them truth, do not deserve kids. Kids that show potential and will take an honest interest in things should receive some help and attention. Just a few suggestions for a train of thought, that would keep it from being the costliest thing that our whole country is involved in and we are doing the worst job of it.

Family life centered around God is the very core of a country. While all our kids cannot all be lying, sleazy, educated, get-rich lawyers that are destroying our country. I know there is a lot to be said about no child left behind, but it did not work things any better for parents, children, or for our government. And certainly, did not save anybody any money. I have strong feelings that myself or no child should be forced to be owned and raised in the belief, religion, and future, or the convenience of any government's lies. God does not say that any government has any opinion of success better than God's teaching.

When I was a very young child, I remember Mystery Babylon making the claim, if you gave them a child at school age, let them raise him for three years, you would never be able to get him to change his beliefs. We give them our children for a lifetime. The great Mother Whore had tried to sink the whole of Europe after they had crucified Jesus, and just about got it done giving themselves and Satan their footing in the world. They had killed well over a hundred-million Christians in around a six to eight-hundred-year period after killing Christ. All in the name of the False-Prophet-Religion, which is the Pope there at Rome. Referred to by John as, "The Great False Prophet, Mother of Harlots and Abominations of the Earth." Now they own our children and through them, the world.

All the purpose is about religion and the Pope being God. They had killed over one hundred million Christian within eight hundred years from the time they killed Christ and most of the Christians there in Europe. God got America built up enough to defeat them in two world wars. America, with God's help saved Europe and the world at least twice. God said, Satan would wear out the saints and rule the world in the last days for a very short time. Can we not see that happening now? Not long ago I would have told you they had a long way to go but look at our schools and government and about anywhere else, it doesn't look very far off any more. And things are moving faster by the day.

I know, I could never save the world, but God has told me all my life that every little bit done for this country toward him will work miracles in these last days, toward making them easier for America. Why I am a full supporter of Trump. Trump is a self-made man and well does his own thinking, and good at it. The liberals do not believe in our *freedom of religion Constitution* (I named them *"God Haters"* around close to forty years ago). Our freedom of religion is one of the greatest things this country owns.

They believe in *freedom from Christ Religion,* and calling it our Constitution. I remember when they would have been like a kid playing with a hangman's noose, saying the things I hear them speaking over the airways today and teaching our children from both houses of Congress. They are not allowed to say the name of "Jesus" in public property. They are doing away with the pledge of allegiance and the name of Jesus. No wonder God says we Christians are asleep.

I thought we fought the battles for our independence to have the freedom to worship God as we please, but now they tell me I can't.

A few people, called Puritans and Pilgrims, that had escaped the Galantine and burning at the stake on top of a brush pile, or pushed off a cliff. Had gotten drove out of Europe by the Mystery Babylon Whore, took their Bibles with them and came to America to establish a colony. They became the beginning of the North American Continent as we know it today, one nation under God. I am fearful that we have lost that standing, and I do not know enough people that can see and hear well enough to ever bring it back to us, because of *education*.

America has given away its soul very cheaply and I am sure will live long enough to regret it. When Jesus starts to pour out the Wrath of God on this earth. (Read your Bible, that is *Jesus* pouring out the Wrath of God on the earth, scorching men with the sun, begging them to repent. Why do you think it is called the wrath of God?) God will have called all his people home to him there in Armageddon, except them that are willing and able to stand and be martyred for the cause of Christ for the great honor of wearing a martyr's crown throughout eternity. They will reign and rule with Christ there from Armageddon for one thousand years.

I would like to place a little-known fact in about here. One cannot show me where in the Bible it says one place that God is going to take his people up to heaven at any time. He is going to bring heaven down to his people. He will be setting in the middle of it. Read your Bible, you might find what it teaches as well as what it does not teach.

After the Mark of the Beast has been taken, it will require one to kill our fleshly bodies to be excepted of the Lord's Spirit. God will not accept a cut-up body operating on a man-made heart and spirit of Lucifer. That is what the "Mark of the Beast" consist of. They want to outlaw and burn our Bibles for it warns of all these things. I do not think they have much to worry about for I hardly know a person that knows how to read the Bible, not even to their children, it has been outlawed. If they let them be sent to the Mystery Babylon Schools, they are hardly allowed to own a

Bible, better not tell anyone about it if you do. This is the way our country is going down.

Thanks to the Devil-possessed Muslim, "Obama," and I cannot say much better about the people who voted for him, they bought and stole the votes to put him in office both times. Didn't I hear Jesus say something about thieves not being able to enter the Kingdom of God? Trump was nothing less than a life-savior for this country, and I do not care if one likes me saying that or not, I do.

Trump would not have been elected if he had not gotten the voting places straightened up a bunch, before the election. The Democrats was sure they had the election sealed up again as usual. It about threw them into shock when Trump won the race. They were so accustomed to thieves winning the election, they were just sure that it was stolen from them. Some of them have not recovered yet, they had to give each other artificial respiration. Hillary has been walking around in a daze for about five months now, trying to find out what happened. Saying that election was hers. Nobody seems to be able to tell her what happened. I suppose she was sleeping again. I may see if I can get her to read one of my books.

Soros and Hollywood's, paid left headed news reporters, can burn in hades for all I care. They can take all their money with them, it will not impress Christ on judgment day or any other day. Christ is a good-deal-maker, but one had better make it with him on this side, he doesn't make good deals, on the other side with people who don't want to know him but want to own him. Like I have already explained, one cannot settle a spiritual debt with carnal money. Hillary does not know that yet. I do not believe any of the politicians do.

Mystery Babylon, (There at Rome) is the beast that is to receive a wound unto death, but will be healed, and will receive more souls than all the other beast, at the end of the world. Under the name of the Antichrist. Every soul whose name is not written in the Lamb's Book of Life will be cast into the lake of fire with her, at the end. All the blood that has been shed on the face of the earth will be avenged upon her, in front of Christ's people, then will be cast alive into the fire that burns forever and ever. Read the seventeenth, eighteenth, and nineteenth chapters of the book of Revelation, for the complete story.

What the world calls education and schooling has done nothing for God's people at any time I know anything about, except full-filing God's Word. They have always worked against God. Including pulling our kids out of our homes, when God told us to teach them there. Can you show me a place in the Bible where God sanctioned a _school_? Although it is not a carnal word, it is mentioned _one_ time in God's Word. I see nowhere God benefited from one or had a good word about one. The schools in Israel, in old testament times, is where most of the false Prophets came from.

When I was a young boy, one of the best Preachers I have personally known, could not read or write when he started out a young man, but he learned it with his wife's help while preaching and baptizing. They sat him in a chair in the pulpit, and he preached his last sermon when he was eighty-eight years old, sounding just as clear as ever. Moses was highly trained in the ways of Pharaoh, Egypt had some of the best schools in the world. It took God forty years of training to get it out of Moses, so he could use him. The Apostle Paul was highly educated, when he was called of God, he said he counted it all as dung. You cannot get much plainer than that.

We were told, around three hundred years ago, schools would be the way Mystery Babylon would take this country over, now they have. It is no wonder God calls us blind and deaf, because we are, and the schools have been working hard to keep us that way. I sometimes think this country has gone beyond redemption. God has said he will spare the life of this country, but he did not say what shape it would be in. Sometimes I wonder.

I had plenty of trouble getting through high school, it was not because I had trouble learning, I could not accept some of the Devilish Junk they had started teaching us in the late nineteen forties and early fifties, I cannot accept it today. Done some schooling in around three different states and some in Europe, had trouble in every one of them. Now that I'll soon be seventy-eight years old, next month on 15, Nov. 2017, I can look at the damage they have done. I would tell them I did not raise myself to believe such lies. Kept me in much trouble.

It was at home I got my raising until I was fifteen years old, that was enough. My mom was a great woman of God, worth more than her weight in gold to me. I could never start in to repay her what I owe her. But Christ can, and I am trying to send up a little Spiritual money for them to use at will.

We seem to not have been told, George Washington that was once named the Father of this country, a tittle that he welled earned. In his farewell speech, warned us to never make a binding treaty with Europe. He could see the danger in his day in what he fought so hard against, that we cannot see even until today.

Mystery Babylon, of Rome, hates our Bible, to them it is bigger than a bull in one's China Closet. No marvel that God says, we are deaf and blind. Education may be one of the greatest things of our time, but what one is teaching in it, is just as important as the teaching itself. More, I think so. Mystery Babylon has succeeded in taking complete charge of this entire country, and don't you ever doubt it. They have done it through Education, just like they told the world they would do. They certainly could not defeat us any other way.

Since they have total charge of our country, they have charge of our education, and own our children. It comes straight from Europe and Mystery Babylon, that finely took over Europe, even after we defeated them in two world wars and every other war we have had with them. I reckon we have just given up. The only way they could ever have taken us. God warned that in the last days that Satan would wear out the Saints, and rule the world for a short time, there would be no flesh left if Christ did not intervene. One might think that the churches are not doing a good enough job, but it lies in the homes not raising their children like Jesus said to raise them, now God will not have them. They are running our churches now. Think on that a minute. They send them to school to be raised, and the schools cannot control them, killing one another, the schools don't want them either.

They started in by convincing us the <u>Bible</u> is a myth, and the most dangerous thing on earth to mankind. Saying it came from an unknown and invisible force that is bent on stealing mankind off the face of the Earth. This is very well happening, because that is what the Bible says will happen. They are disappearing every day to prove it right.

The other things it has said is coming, will come, especially the Judgment Day. One can never argue against that? They say, Mystery Babylon is here to save us all and deliver us from the clutches of the Bible and its doctrine which is sure death. Part of their message is true, but where are they going to save us to? I believe there is more mystery in their doctrine than there ever was in the Bible. Maybe that is the reason God named them Mystery Babylon. Seems that is a very fitting name to me. I do not know why it cannot catch the interest of every sane man, that has eyes and ears. I guess I was not put here to figure everything out.

But I can read my Bible and I have not found one thing wrong in it yet, I cannot say that about any other book I have read. The only mistake I know of that God made was man, he repented of that, and is going to fix it. He has told us all things, but we are very hard of hearing. Many of us have selective hearing, and want to believe anything but truth, even coming up with a world-saying, <u>truth</u>-<u>hurts</u>. I don't doubt that it does, but more truth is the only antidote that is guaranteed. Mystery Babylon, has gotten to be maybe the biggest man organization on earth, and is going to get bigger. Has pushed its education plan over on America by outlawing the Bible and the name Jesus Christ, that Christians are named after, and we are not allowed to say his name in a Babylon School or on any government property. Which includes about every school in our country and our armed services, they all teach the Babylon Doctrine.

The Babylon Doctrine demands that every state give their children to Babylon at the age of six and they own them from there on out. The home only gets them by the rules and permission of Mystery Babylon, as they specify. If they do not comply, the children will be taken from the home and placed in another home specified by Mystery Babylon. They will instruct the new family on what they can do with the children and how they are to handle them and how they are to educate them. Education is how they got them in the first place, and for sure is the only way they are going to own and keep them.

No one will be allowed to educate them in anything else, certainly not from the Bible. It gives death to any government, or man, taking the place of God in this world. If God's people will stand up against them with the Bible, they are dead. They cannot allow for anyone to teach them from the Bible, if they know how to teach it; it will preach them into hell. So, this government gives death to God if one opens a mouth contrary to anything they say. It is called politicianly correct. The Bible is not allowed anywhere in a government building or property when Democrats are running things, they are atheist clear through and converting the rest of the world to them. Do you wonder why I do not think much of the Democrats? Read them two paragraphs again.

They have been known to fire a school teacher just for having a small New Testament in her possession on school property. A navy Champlin was court-marshalled and thrown out of the services, under Obama, for saying the name Jesus Christ while in a uniform. They have removed "<u>So help me God</u>" from the pledge to our flag. Obama ordered the Bibles removed from the drawers in hotel rooms around one big army fort. I could fill this page with unbelievable things our government has done. There is no limit to what Devil possessed people will do, if they can get away with it. I've never known one of them to promote fairness or a clean fight if they had any reason to think they could get away with otherwise. Their domain is just as big as they can control with all the force of their lies and dirty tricks they can use. And no limit to what Christians will swallow whole while they are asleep. No marvel that God says for us to wake up.

God teaches, there is a few things we owe our worst enemies. One of them is to not let ourselves get down to their level. I for one, believe that I have permission from God for self-defense, for me and my family and possessions. Our laws and courts are set and run by Mystery Babylon, so a Christian is not to expect a Christian trial in a Babylon Court even though our country and laws were started out and built on God's Word. Babylon Education has taken care of that, and scattered it to heck and gone, this is what this book is meant to be about. A Mystery Babylon court was the one that sentenced Jesus to death. They have not quit and have no intention of ever quitting. God warned it would be a battle as long as we have time.

I am far from them that preach, we must lay down and roll over if the Devil decides to act a little tough. Apparently, that preacher has not read his Bible very close, maybe not at all. He must have received his Education from Mystery Babylon, I've heard a lot of them.

I preach we should get back to preaching from the King James Authorized Bible, the one *"Jesus said he wrote"* around the year sixteen-hundred AD. All the Bible writings of the world was screened and used by him, all he thought he needed. And said plainly he did not want a word in it moved or changed. How much plainer could he have gotten? If one word in it has been changed, it is not his Word anymore. And they cannot label it with the original King James Label, it's against the law. Show me another book that has been over the world for a thousand-years and one cannot show me one word in it that has been altered. And I will show you a miracle. Some people think age is a way to rate a book, I fail to see the connection.

I am lately amazed at how powerful Jesus Christs' words really are. He was the Word that was with God in the beginning, he spoke this whole creation into beginning. Borne himself into human flesh, came and walked this earth as an ordinary man then suffered death for our sacrifice. Went back to the father and sent back, unto the entire world, their Spirit to dwell in every human being that would be reborn into his Spirit. He would save them forever to be with him in a new, heaven, earth and body. It is bigger than our imagination. That is Spiritual talk, carnal cannot believe it. I do not Know a single word that he has not covered in his Word and hardly a person will give him the time of day unless they want him to give them more. How long do you think he will stand and knock at each one of our heart's door? We do not have a smidgen of a thought toward how great he really is. Where can one find a carnal Jesus like that to preach?

Mystery Babylon, (The world), teaches our children, *they* are the real god and are here to save us from the God of the Bible. I was not real surprised at the world believing them, but I used to have the faith in this country being taught better than that. God has warned us it will be a rough battle and if we are not prepared to fight, we will lose our very souls. I am starting to see what he means, and very well know it is going to get much worse. We are barely started into, "The beginning of sorrows that Jesus told us about." Babylon that is destined to rule the world and slay all Christians is starting to rise to its calling.

We should always keep in mind God has told us all things. But it is a must we are to keep reading our Bible, it contains every word God has said to us. When one can accept that, it is a mighty big step toward knowing Jesus Christ, the Savior. He is the Spirit of God, the Word, the Bible, the Truth, the Life, and everything else. We are complete in him. He is the Education you hear many talking about, but few ever heard the words, "Spiritual Education." That, being Spiritual, would all be in the King James Bible, nowhere else. Every word in it is Spiritual, every word not in it is a carnal word.

The reason so many people do not see and know God the creator, he is a Spirit. Most people do not know enough about the Spirit to know the spirit they have in them. Spirit is the life in anything that has life in it. We are led by the spirit that we cater to. People commit mass murder and cannot explain why, because they do not know their own spirit. We should get to know the spirit that is directing us. We should know our own thoughts that is running around in our minds. These are the spirits that are leading us. We should be teaching our children of them. If we don't read our Bible we will not know how or why.

I have written before, I do not know a part of our body that can be identified as our spirit any better than our mind, and maybe the parts it controls. Seems to me if one would keep a clean, clear, mind, one could keep out of serious trouble. It stands to reason if we cannot practice keeping in control of our minds and keep it on good things, who knows when the Devil himself might decide to take it over. He is a spirit, God calls him the tempter. I know he don't give up easy, and never gives up completely, long as he is given a spot to dwell in. He has always played a heavy part in God's creation and is still playing a great part. God has given us a very plain revelation of him and has named his allotted-time and warned us all about him and his end. Without God's help, we are no match for him, but we are promised his help if we will come to know and trust God. He will not fail us.

One doesn't much more than get started reading God's Word, till you can see God, man, and the Devil. They are all well-carried through the Word and record that God gives to us of the time of man, and his existence on this earth. We each should keep in mind, we are only given a short amount of time comparable to maybe one inch of small thread on a very big ball of it rolled up. We can only play that small a part on the full roll, but we will be going into eternity with the part we play. With eternity past at one end and eternity future at the other. Least we fail to consider God is the one in total control of the entire thing and told us all things. Including, if we can be happy to love and embrace him to guide us, we can move into eternity with him, or else oblivion with Satan, choice is ours.

Requirements are to love and trust his Son, Jesus Christ. I have decided to accept him and have enjoyed it ever since. But each person must clear his thinking from carnal things, they will eat one like a cancer. May be the reason God gave us cancer to deal with that we will not forget. I say this whole thing is a mind thing. After all the mind is our Spirit, we are told to align it with God's Spirit, they both are the life in one, might as well tie them together. There is no other way to possess them.

2

MORE ON ("THE MARK OF THE BEAST")

IN THE BOOK OF Revelations, that Jesus gave to John, while on the thirteen-square mile rock the Bible calls the Isle of Patmos. John was told to write it down, he did. Everything past the forth chapter of Revelations is written from heaven, and how it is seen from there by the Spuirit. John saw an Angel, flying in the midst, of heaven, having the everlasting gospel to preach unto them that dwell on the earth, ever nation, and kindred, and tongue, and people. That included every man on the earth.

The first mention of the Mark of the Beast can be found in the thirteenth chapter of the book of revelations, one of the books that John wrote. It is identified as a mark in the forehead or in one's hands, the name of the beast, or the number of his name. It is the number of a man. God teaches, man power without God, is a beast.

Anyone should be able to establish every word with at least two or three reliable witnesses before it is repeated as gospel, even the Word of God. With God that is a verifying number, if the witnesses are from the Word of God. He also says, every word from the mouth of God should be established the same way.

This, being soundly and thoroughly practiced, would eliminate every denomination but one on the earth. It would be the established Word of God, by the Word of God. That is making it equal to the Bible, in the Language of the Spirit. That would be a mighty powerful scripture. Like the King James has had done to it and all of it can be gone over repeatedly if one has not fooled with it. Like change a word in it, which Jesus said not to do.

No man can know how much power the Word of God can contain, until it is practiced. I believe any man, could and would, be amazed, if he watched any of it fully put to work. It created the heavens and the earth. No way I know of watching it but reading and believing the Word of God. I've heard awfully little of it being preached or taught in any such way in my short seventy-eight years of life here. I do not know why, unless it is because I do not know one denomination that could hold up to that kind of preaching. Any preacher would find himself without a denomination in a short while, to preach the Word very strong, then who would support him? Ask me, I can tell you. The answer is God, if one is walking close to God, God will be there. But few denominations would be.

Education in this country is so scared of the Word of God, they have passed laws that forbids the Word of God to be spoken *about* in our schools. But they claim to be teaching the value of *unity*. If they are, they are sure not doing a very good job of teaching. God is the author of the teaching of unity, and they have outlawed mentioning him in the schoolhouse, putting themselves above God. Why would any denominational preacher, want to preach his own denomination out of church? That is the reason a denomination is a doomed organization, if they will not hear the Word of God they will remain dead.

Divided people are a spiritually dead bunch of people, and if you wonder why I do not belong to any certain group of people, that should answer your question. I do not know of one that I could belong to, as a preacher, without agreeing to preach *their* beliefs. I only preach, as gospel, what I can explain and establish from the King James Authorize Translation, with two and three establishing witnesses from the Word of God. I do not know a denomination that will fully agree to or live up to that.

They may say they do, but have they been tested? They will have to agree to it, are at least to listen to me preach it to them, so I just do not bother them as far as making an allegiance with them. I know, it doesn't make one a lot of Christian friends. I never did desire a lot of attention, but sometimes feel like a magnet, at drawing a lot of negative attention, namely our country. Of course, Christ has plainly warned us of that, he said the world would try to have us put to death. Look around you and over the world. Listen to the news, they are being killed every day, of the year.

I am always free to set down and listen to them, and let them present their view, even though I may not fully agree with them. I will set down with them with my Bible and present to them my beliefs, with the establishing scriptures, if they want to hear them. I do not find very many people that ever heard of the scripture that says, every word is to be established by at least two or three witnesses, even the Word of God, and never heard anyone preaching it. It is in the Bible several places, one is 2nd Corinthians, thirteen, and one. Another is Matthew, eighteen and verse six. If two have the same amount of three witnesses, but establishing it differently, which I have never heard of, somebody is reading it wrong. Then a jury, called the congregation or elders, is to decide which one of them sounds the more likely correct. God has set that up in his laws. The Bible is to decide ever issue, it interprets the Bible.

I have been advised by editors concerning my writings, one said I should verify all my statements to make the people believe I know what I am talking about. That is good advice I am sure, but it causes me some bit of a problem trying to do that. Every new word I come across, I'd try to write a few pages to explain it by the way I was using it, that ended up with me writing books about my books. I hope I'm improving, it is written in all my books that the Bible is the only source I use, to prove my statements. If one doesn't believe the Bible, he will not believe my books for sure. God has said, if one does not believe the record he has given us of his son, he will not be accepted as one of His. That is recorded in the Bible.

It takes a lot of time in studying and verifying, but that is about all I do any more. It has been quite an experience, so far. The King James Authorize Translation is my measuring stick on anything. It built and established this nation. In my opinion it is the truth, the whole truth, nothing but the truth. This is what our country used to swear on, for anything legal and official, before we got so smart and accepted the *government* for our God and the only thing that must be accepted as correct, in other words *politically correct*. But just look at the shape political correctness, has this country in. They can forget it as far as I am concerned, I do not think politics has ever been correct for a whole day in its life.

Political correct, just means that lying politicians are in charge, and have the total control to say what is right or wrong. That is what they gain if they can disregard the Bible and the reason they hate the Bible. If that doesn't wake one up, no wonder my Bible says we are deaf, blind, and have no life in us. Have you met a politician that can promise you eternal life? No government is above God in God's chain of command.

God has said, when a people like that ask me for help, I will tell them to ask the gods they are serving, for help. Look at the people in this world that needs help and thinks our government owes it to them. They are going to the wrong God, it's that simple.

Satan is getting the world set up to take the "Mark of the Beast." Against the "Spirit Written Language" of this world. That is one of the things I was intending to write this book about, it is a big story. But, like I just wrote I'm having difficulty staying with it as the subject. I know now what my mother was talking about, seventy-four years ago. When she would be churning for butter in the old stone churn and talking of it <u>coming together</u>. There may not be many old enough left to understand that remark, but it sounds appropriate to me at the age of seventy-eight years. Hopefully, when I finish I'll have every corner gathered and covered.

I know there has been a lot of other good books written, called Bibles and scriptures, but I do not know of a one that Jesus claims to be him, written by the Holy Spirit itself, Jesus Christ. The King James Authorized Translation, makes that claim, I believe it has proved it. Jesus told all his people to preach it to the Greek and the Hebrew, and to ever creature on the earth. I know, people that tell me I must be schooled in the understanding of Greek and Hebrew, to preach. I disagree with them.

I do not believe I have read where the Greek and Hebrew have been told to preach their Bible to the English-Speaking people. The King James Translation is the only true, complete, history book of mankind, about the past, present, and the future that I've ever read. We did not have it until around sixteen-hundred AD. Before then we had Moses and the Prophets. I have not found one lie or one slanted remark in it and it is completed. It has condemned any man to hell that won't believe and love the truth, and says, it is the Truth, Jesus Christ.

Any man that has no contact with the Spirit, has no contact with life. Jesus has said, "He" is the door, the way, the truth, the life, the very breath we have, he breaths it into us. If he takes it back from us we will go back to the dust of the Earth, where we came from. That does not give man much authority to himself. The only reason a man with any common sense cannot see it all is, he has willingly accepted blindness, by Satan. And unwilling to accept the, freely given, Spirit of God. Which is the King James Authorized Translation of the Bible; the Word of God, which is the Truth, Jesus Christ, the only mediator between man and God.

The carnal flesh and spirit of man despises the Spirit of God and has declared war on God and anything that belongs to God and is *"dead set"* on fighting it until the death, I do not know why. God's Spirit is the only ounce of life the flesh has in it. This dead condition is surely; *"The Mark of the Beast."* It is a condition inside one's body, put there by man.

God is not going to die, and man has only been given seventy years, with probably a few million ways to shortening that, and a few ways he might lengthen it a little. It is plain we are to accept (Or press) our way into the Spirit, if we intend to make it into eternal life and the new heaven and earth. Then work to make our calling and election sure. For we will not make the crossing with these fleshly bodies. They will not be needed in heaven, and God will never allow them in. They must die to accept the Spirit of God which is life itself.

Jesus has laid himself out in Word Form, called the King James Translation, that I call *"The Spirit Language of God"* it is the only writing of the Spirit I know of on this earth. Jesus said he wrote it, it is him. I have fully learned to believe God and trust him to the high heaven, from the smallest creeping thing to the last peddle of a flower. He spoke the creation into existence, with his Word from the Mouth of God. Mankind is struggling to believe that, for it is above his comprehension without help. Just look around you, it is there. Man has been trying to explain it to himself for six-thousands years. I believe Adam knew more about creation in his day than our top scientist knows today. Can you imagine Adam fully comprehending the mast size and further happenings of the earth he was standing on? God gave us a lesson that we have not fully received as yet. A man should never hear a woman over God.

Man is an amazingly complicated piece of machinery created and operated by the Spirit of God and given the power to reproduce himself and a free will. Works very well if we will just let God do the leading. From the beginning man has sought to take total control of himself and everything around him in every way. He has made much progress in these last few years, so he thinks, but will never be able to attain complete control until he can overpower God. He will never do that. Lucifer tried that once, with a third of God's created beings helping him.

Man's age started out being close to a thousand years old in the beginning of man on this earth. After about three shortening downs, God cut man's time to live on this earth down to seventy years old, in King David's time, around three to four thousand years ago. With all of man's success and accomplishments added together man has not added one year to his average length of life since it was shortened down for mankind's sake in David's time, though he thinks he has. Man can figure his average age in around years today, but he cannot read and believe the Bible. When it is right ever time.

God has named and describe the total beginning and end to all mankind, and most of everything in between, with some help from Adam. Man was built and blessed with a great desire and ambition to take control of everything on the earth. God has given him a free will and charge of all things, then he gave him woman to show him he is not very well adapted to take charge of everything. He must depend upon the Lord to help him. He must not cross someone else's same freedom that he has and acknowledge God as the head.

This was one of God's common-sense laws as well as an order.

Man turned out with such a provocative, greedy nature, God was forced to intervein. After Adam had given the whole creation to the Devil. He has no intention of saving mankind in the shape man has gotten himself into. Man is destined to annihilate himself, with the desires for himself to sit in God's seat.

God is a jealous God. His intention is to save only a few out of all mankind to be with him forever. Those who have overcome their provocative nature and learned to let God lead them. He will have no other kind.

If you are not happy here with God being the head, do not expect him to take you to be with him forever. I do not believe that to be a bullish attitude considering how plain an explanation he has given to us. And what he has plainly spoken and offered to prepare for mankind that can love his righteousness. If a man will not love and receive righteousness in his short tenner here, he will be destroyed in hell. Might remember that, the next time you start complaining and griping to God with an eager to ignore him.

It is the same Spirit in us now as it will be that will be operating in us throughout eternity. If we will align it with the Spirit of God, or else it will align you with the Antichrist. If we cannot acknowledge God's Spirit as the head here, how will we love it on the other side? It is a righteous Spirit, God will tolerate nothing else to be with him. One third of the spirits that God created, rebelled and left God, we have that for an example. If we accept their spirit here, they will be the ones we will spend eternity with. God has prepared a hell for them to be destroyed in.

It is the spirit of each person that will determine where one spends eternity. There are only two sides for one to align his spirit with, one is the Spirit of God, the other is the spirit of Lucifer. God will have nothing to do with the spirit of Lucifer, or the Devil, not many will be totally free from the spirit of Satan. We are to have a heart constantly full of prayer and repentance with a humble sincere contrite Spirit before God always. God always looks at us through the heart and always sees and knows every bit of us. He is about the spirit he calls his. He does not claim just any spirit that says, Lord, Lord.

I can assure you if spirits are torturing you here, they are not the spirits that God's Spirit has sent to us. Even though it is a practice of mankind to blame God with everything that is unpleasant to his own carnal nature, they are aligned with the one-third that Michael kicked out of heaven and you are believing and catering to them. They do not love anything that is righteous. God's Word tells us of a better Spirit, we must believe and accept him to see it. Carnality cannot see a spirit, we must believe the Spirit of God. God says every Word of his is Truth, but man's word is a lie unless it aligns with what God says, then it is God's Word. The only Spirit of God we can have that will save us.

We are each given a spirit of our own and are told to train it up in the fear and admonition of the Lord and let the Spirit of God lead us, it will never lead us against the Word of God which is the King James Authorized Translation of the Bible. Jesus, gave it to England, around sixteen-hundred AD, said it was him in Word form. He does not want a word changed or nothing taken from a word in it. If it has, then it is not God's Word. I intend to write more on this in this book.

It is the only thing on earth that is going into heaven unchanged when Christ Comes back for his. It is the Spiritual Language of Words that can be found in the King James Translation of the Bible, it is Christ. One can ride them through the complete change, all the way over but he must be born again into the Spirit of God. The carnal cannot have that and will stay in the carnal world. And will forever be locked out from the presents of the Father. Any religion that does not believe in, and accept the born-again experience, is just a false religion, falling short of the glory of God.

I write a lot about being led by the Spirit, it is what the Bible is about. God demands it, without any doubt it calls for us to come to know something about the Spirit of God. Without it, we are referred to by our creator as being dumb, blind, dead, lost, and without hope, and many other things, like having been turned over to our lust after carnal things. His Spirit cannot be obtained without some studying, believing, and receiving. We cannot be saved without it. I have done much of all them and would like to share some of it with you.

The best I can figure out, the spirit is the same thing in our bodies as the brain and nervous system, making up our minds. Together, they operate and control our entire body, giving us complete responsibility for our decisions and actions if we have a sound Godly mind. *Sound* implies, not having any holes and hollow spots in it and having a firm foundation under it, like two good feet and strong legs and can stand against opposition, with a sound voice.

Speaking of man's education, I have been hearing, from reliable sources, that our scientists have about gotten a mechanical system ready to start installing into all human beings. They say it can outperform all the things that a normal human can do. Think, plan, see-ahead, and make choses and decisions from its own will. If you don't believe that, then tell me who the people are that are running to the mountains, praying for the rocks and mountains to fall on them and hide them from the face of "The one that is sitting on the throne," told about there in Revelations. When Jesus is pouring out God's wrath upon the earth trying to get, what is left of mankind, to repent and receive the Spirit of God.

It is certainly not God's Spirit-filled people. But death will flee from them for a five-month period. Jesus is pleading with them, with his wrath of torcher, to repent. Even though it will mean death to the carnal, man-created, body that has received the Mark of a Man, when they do. Jesus will be set in Jerusalem with his saints and the Jews ruling the earth with an iron hand. It is not any different from the agreement we've had with God all along.

The carnal flesh has always been required to die-out, for God to be accepted into his Spirit. This Mark of the Beast is a covenant to accept the Mark of a Man permanently, and death to withdraw from it, spiritually speaking. If the flesh would die out now, we could go on living, but the Spirit of God is to have complete control over the flesh. If it doesn't, then we are none of Gods. The Mark of the Beast is a contract for the flesh to not do that; then it must physically die to receive the Spirit of God. One cannot have the Spirit of God and the Mark of the Beast in the same body. That is plainly in the Bible, though I have never heard it preached.

My Bible speaks of such a creature, calls it the "Mark of the Beast." I am getting a book published now written on this subject, calling it by tittle, revealing the "Mark of the Beast." Can be bought anywhere books are sold. Don't expect me to explain how it works but I can say a few words on how the body works and these scientists will have to build a computer to control a man's thinking, or his mind, to accomplish this project. Our thinking, controls our spirit and our body. Our mind controls our thinking. It is hard to tell what someone without a sound mind, or double minded is thinking, he is unstable for sure. The Bible says a double minded man is unstable in all his ways.

The spirit is the life of anything that has life in it. When the spirit has left something, it is dead, dead. These scientists know, to put life into anything, they must come up with a spirit, so they have been working twenty-four-seven to come up with a computer that will replace a spirit. Since they cannot create a spirit in anything, they will use one's spirit and one's mind to control the computer while it is controlling the mind. Called the "Mark of the Beast" (Man without God is a beast) I can see no better way to explain it. It is kind of like a dog chasing its tail, around and around, think they can have it winning? They think so.

God says this will, in a short time, put an end to all normal flesh. God will not accept any such people that has accepted a man-made spirit, made and controlled by man's hands and the spirit of Lucifer. Man must deny this spirit and accept the Spirit of God. If one accepts this "Mark of the Beast" it will be accepting the death penalty for our bodies. God teaches this. He is told he will never die. Can you imagine believing that?

If one lives down to the time, of the rule of the Antichrist, he gives one the choice to take the mark or he will take your head. One might as well give him their head, in the end it will be the same thing either way. The majority, of people today have been taught they do not need the Spirit of God. Kind of pitiful any way one can describe it, if they do not receive the Spirit of God they have no real life in them, just an image of the real thing.

This is the same deal from the beginning. When Adam and Eve disobeyed God, they died, God has tried to find a way to reconcile man back to him ever since. Man is looking for a way to bar Christ (Which is God) out of any control of his body. This Mark will be it, but a fatal move for the body.

The "Mark of the Beast" is introduced in the thirteenth chapter of Revelations. It, and the next three chapters, will about cover the very end times up to the time of God's wrath. When the last seven-years-week, of the seventy-years of weeks told about in Daniel, is poured out on the earth. God will have turned back to the Jews with his saints, ruling from Jerusalem. It seems to me like the only way for anyone to receive the Spirit after one has taken this mark, is to give his body as a sacrifice for it.

I believe, from the writings, that the ones that has accepted Christ by this time, went with him back to the Jews. Like he told about in the twenty-forth chapter of the book of Matthew. The closest thing I can find in my Bible to what man calls a rapture, but they are only going to Armageddon, in the hills around Jerusalem. They had accepted being a Jew when they accepted Christ. Seems very plain, that this consists of much more than the today's average Christians wants to accept or hear anything about. I write often, "Read your Bible" and could write it more often, for it is important for one to verify this.

We do not see much deep studying of the Bible in the way God said to study it. This has become much more important to God in these last days, and less important to man. Mostly because of man's so many inventions and fast and free living that man has chosen for himself and does not have time for God. Until he gets to thinking he has passed God up and God is just kind of getting in man's way. God has said plainly,

"Whosoever exalts himself, shall be abased." God teaches that very few will make it through these last days and stay saved. I believe he teaches at the very end there will not be a one left alive and saved in the earth, except the ones that are with him and the Jews there at Jerusalem, called Armageddon. When God saves any Gentile, he will take him home at that time. The Antichrist world will make sure of that.

Christ is accepting the Jews for they have cried out for him to save them, and they have accepted him, while the gentiles have accepted the Antichrist and have killed the ones that will not. And had went after the Jews to kill them, Christ came back to save them. The Mark of the Beast is the final straw to living and controlling your own body.

Christ has said death is more blessed than the mark. Accepting Christ now, is better than either one. I was hoping and praying more earnest-preachers would give the Mark of the Beast a more deeper study. As it is very possible that a few children born today may be living in the day of the Mark of the Beast. It is for sure their great, grandchildren will be. They sure can use some more in-depth information to help them to keep our country as free from it as possible. Our country is the only one we can save, we can only preach to any others. I believe Christ has said it is time we started preaching it, and from the Bible. Instead of so much preaching on how talented and comfortable man's inventions are than what God gives to us. Satan has taken over their message. That preacher is preaching for the Antichrist, not Christ.

Trump is a man sent from God to give this nation a chance to turn back to God. Trump cannot save it, but he is there to give us a chance to turn back to Jesus while we still can, if we want to. The Devil would give his eye teeth to impeach Trump, listen to them Devil possessed Democrats across the country crying out. I strongly believe that Trump is this country's last chance. Seems to me that the dumbest man on this earth should be able to see that if he has one Spiritual eye, but God has said we are fools and blind, and we go on every day proving him right.

I started to write, I cannot understand that, but that would be wrong, I spent thirty some-odd years wrapped up in sin before I received Christ forty years ago and have not been sorry for one minute of it since. I even used to be a Democrat.

That is the way I was heavily raised, until I received the Spirit of God. I have not been a Democrat since. I not only gave up many things of the world, I gave up all the world and everything in it. I believe that was a good trade, for eternal life with God. And it's looking like, with my whole family, I am promised just that. He has saved my children and all my grandchildren from the world many times. It is looking favorable that they will all be saved when they leave this world.

The last seven years' week, will Lead up to the millennial reign, when Christ will set-up his kingdom there in Jerusalem for the millennial reign. Then the

earth will have a perfect rule for a thousand years
coming from Jesus Christ, with his martyrs and his
saints ruling with him for one thousand years. And
will have time to replenish much of the earth under
Jesus' rule. The False Prophet and the Antichrist will
have been thrown into hell and the Devil will be bound
in the pit in chains of darkness with a thousand-year
seal upon him. Every person will have a chance to love
a perfect rule under Christ. Christ did all that when
he came back to save the Jews from Mystery Babylon,
there at Rome. That will cover some of the wars Jesus
talked about. The beginning of them are already going
on. The people who are looking for a rapture are going
to be dispointed.

The Devil will be released after the thousand-year
reign, to prepare ever nation for the great battle of
Armageddon, also called the day of the Great Battle
of God Almighty. This will be the final weeding-out
time.

Christ will release the Devil from his one thousand
years in chains of darkness, to gather the people that
hate righteousness and is dissatisfied with Christ's
perfect rule, from ever kingdom on the earth to defeat
Christ and his small camp of saints there in Jerusalem.
Where Christ has been ruling with an iron hand. They
have had need of nothing but power and authority over
themselves to do as they please, they think. They should
know that has never worked. Christ took over to keep
them from ending all flesh, to save the ones that loves

righteousness. You can look over the world today and see how few that is going to be. They love self instead.

The Devil will convince them that are left, they can defeat Jesus easily, with the largest army every gathered on the earth. Christ's little group probably don't even have a gun. Believe me, Christ has been rough on the world's people, trying to get them to repent, and receive the Spirit of God. Them that know Christ, will not need a gun, they have Christ. It will be called the battle of Armageddon. Also called the day of the Great Battle of God Almighty.

God will have judged the earth but will set up the white throne judgment to reward every person for their works, good or bad. Christ will throw Satan into the lake of fire where the False Prophet and the Antichrist already are. (You need not look for them as a man, they are a spirit with many possessed people). Along with every soul that does not have its name written in the Lamb's Book of Life. The final separation. Christ will burn up the entire creation except the ones that are prepared to spend eternity with him.

This will make up the complete Mystery Babylon Whore, every soul that does not have its name written in the Lambs Book of Life is listed in the books of Mystery Babylon. Taken over by the Antichrist, called even the eighth kingdom on the earth for one hour and is of the seven, namely Rome with its ten horns. Like a cage filled with every foul spirit and every unclean and hateful bird on the earth. Notice when the Angel announces in the eighteenth-chapter of Rev. that

Babylon is fallen, Babylon is fallen, he has dropped the word, Mystery. I do not believe there is any Mystery left about it at that time. Of course, it never was a mystery to God or God's people that have gotten to know God and his Word.

The whole creation is going to be burned up. There, the Bible starts talking about the new heavens and earth appearing. (Quoting from the Bible) I want to think that every word of this book is taken from the Bible.

If you think we have seen wars and rumors of war, people killing people, and families betraying one another, and all the other things that Jesus talked about. Like the sun being blackened, earthquakes like we've never seen before, rivers turning to blood. All matter of men, small and great, hiding in and calling to the rocks and mountains to fall on them to hide them from the face of the one on the throne. Jesus will be among men again, begging them to repent and receive the Spirit of God. Even though it will mean death to the bodies Marked with a Beast Mark.

The sun scorching men, for a five-month period where men will seek to die but death will flee from them. Jesus pouring out his wrath of torcher on all the earth, pleading with mankind, what is left of them, to repent. But Jesus said they would be blaming him for the plagues, cursing him and would not repent. He must have been referring to the majority or a certain time, for in another place around close to the same time, he mentioned many did repent.

I'm allowed to tell us now, at-this-time we haven't seen anything yet. Wait until the seven-year week of Jesus pouring out his wrath, referred to all up threw the Bible that it is coming. We are nearing times that most of us cannot imagine and no one has seen times like these before, and man will never see times like them again. Jesus saying death in the Lord will be a blessing, from here on out. If you are already with him at Jerusalem and have not received the Mark is the only safe place to be.

One of my main purposes for writing this book was to expose the Bible to the generation that is coming into this spot in history. They are going to need it badly. Very few of them living today, if any, will be involved in this week but the ones we are to prepare for it.

Jesus said for us to pray that we would be found worthy to stand before him and not go through these things. Sounds mighty much like he is saying that death in Jesus, wherever he is at, would be better than living in these times. Receiving his Spirit would be receiving death to the carnal body that has receive the Mark of a Man. I am convinced that I am standing before Jesus now, every day. Some people think they will require a rapture. Carefully read Mathew twenty-four. Don't miss the line – "Jesus gathering up all his elect from the four winds of the earth." Matt. Twenty-four the thirty first verse.

He did name a point in time to John and told him to write it down. He also mentioned a time in the Old Testament where he said God was calling his people home and no one was taking it to heart. But I have never read where I will have to wait on or pray for a rapture. I've said before, it's not that I do not believe there is a rapture, just not one like the big boys are preaching. I suppose it is owing to what one calls a rapture. The word is not one of God's words.

I do not find the word in my Bible, nor one that it replaces, nor one that replaces it. So, it is a carnal word rather than a Spiritual one. I prefer to just leave it alone, rather than try to build one up that is not there. A word that would need established by two and three witnesses from God's Word. I do not see that Jesus needed any of my help to write the Bible. I am sure if he would have needed that word, he would have put it in there when he wrote the Bible.

I would not want to throw one of you rapture preachers into shock, but I have not found one place in the Bible where it says any one person will leave this earth and go to heaven. Maybe someone can show it to me.

Man's mind is small, weak, foolish, and flimsy when it is compared to a Spirit, or the Word of God, but try to tell that to a carnal mind. He will probably want to give one a demonstration, free of charge. I have not found a Bible statement to be wrong yet. The Bible is the Spirit of God in spiritual word form. I do believe it is high time for the ones who claim to be Christians to awake and see you can trust the Bible completely, and far, far, above any college professor that knows what God meant to say or can read in Greek or Hebrew.

Paul said so plainly, and words that *man* has built up I do not care for.

Like everything else God made, our mind is made with two sides. We have the carnal side and the spiritual side. If Satan is allowed, he will take total control of the carnal side and kill all the spiritual side he possibly can. He is carnal and knows it very well, without the Spirit of God, which is the King James Bible, no man is a match for Satan and his imps. He is there for no other reason but to kill, steal and destroy anything of mankind, but Satan's spirits are scared to death of Jesus the Spirit of God.

Satan never sleeps, in that aspect he is like God and can appear as an angel of light, and sing like a Mocking Bird, he has his own built-in musical instruments. He is seeking whom he may devour. God says he is beautiful, everything about him is to deceive mankind. God referred to him as the god of this world. Given that position by mankind.

He is a never-ending battle, actual war, with mankind, until Jesus throws him into the eternal lake of fire along with every soul whose name is not written in the "Lamb's Book of Life." The world seems to be full of high-pressured, fast-talking, pushy-salesmen, trying to put words in your mouth then get you to sign off on them. A Christian has no part with such people. I've never seen a case that I needed one of them to be on my side for me. Satan and his imps must rank around the top of that heap. One sure needs to learn to pick them out. But be careful, God has been known to use Satan himself to deliver his people.

Satan's people delivered Jesus to the cross, to the will of God. I have written much in other books, the only way I know one to be able to be sure, is to know the spirit you are dealing with, and the spirit you are dealing from. Too heck with judging the deed, just be with the Spirit of God at the end. That is Jesus Christ in person. He will judge every deed, the Bible says he is busy judging every day, everybody will receive a fair deal.

Experience is a wonderful teacher, but it is usually very expensive and costly. One cannot live long learning by too many mistakes or by experience all the time. Better look around and learn by other's mistakes or read some decent books like the Bible. They do not cost one so much and you will live longer by believing it, might even learn to enjoy life.

God says to try the spirits, you can study your Bible and do that without gambling so many high stakes. Whether they know it or not, everybody tends to mess with someone else's mind, but only an evil spirit will do it just for his own gain and your loss. Why God uses the word, *mind*, so much in his Word. He even told us we could have the mind of Jesus Christ. As a fact, he recommended it strongly. We will need to fit our mind with it. Not the other way around.

Life itself is somewhat of a gamble, we should learn the Spirit of Truth, it is the only sure-thing in this world that is a sure-thing every time. It pays to get to know the Spirit. If it is the Spirit of God it is a sure-thing; if it is a sure-thing, it is the Spirit of God. If it is not the Spirit, it is just an image. The dictionary says carnal is anything apart from the Spirit. God says anything carnal is dead and just an image of the Spirit, including our fleshly bodies.

The (Spirit Language; Bible) is the same one God confused from the earth to divide mankind all over the earth. Scattering mankind worked well but it has served its purpose, God is ready to bring them back together. The ones that are ready to unite with God instead of contrary to God. In other words, the other side of our minds and going the other direction.

I do not believe it is out of line to believe the first language that the whole earth spoke, before God confused it from the earth, probably did not make a sound. Something like we call telepathic. But God confused that language from the earth and every creature had to learn to communicate with other like creatures. A spirit and animals still speak it. That not only divided humans, it put a divide between man and animal creatures and creeping things. God said the Serpent was subtler than all the others. A dragon is more than apt a serpent, before God took his legs from him, and sentenced him to crawl on his belly.

Jesus says his Spirit is the Life, the Truth, the Light and everything else a man needs to survive. God divided the world by confusing the one language they had, he will unite them together again by restoring it back to the ones that will hear and believe his one

Spiritual Language of the Bible. All spirits are not of God. It is a must to hold them together again and as one with God. This is what I intended this book to be about. A language between man and God, the Mark of the Beast is undoubtable a language but not one I would care to buy into.

Every word should be established with two and three witnesses from God's Word, this is a Spiritual Language. Christ says he does not receive a testimony from man, God does not need nor, will he receive anything carnal unless it is born-again and made new. Every word that is not found in the King James Authorized Bible is a carnal word and is to be established from the Bible that Jesus wrote, as truth or as a lie. That includes any other language.

Everything is what it is, depending on where you are looking at it from. The carnal and the Spirit are backwards to one another, they see things from opposite sides, and are going in opposite directions. This would explain a lot as to the disagreement between Christians and people of the world, they are not looking at things from the same position. Or better said, from the same Spirit. There is to be no spiritual divisions among God's people. They are all one in the Spirit of God.

One will only understand that, by faith alone. Faith is believing, God is a Spirit and says you cannot please him without faith. Paul called us a new creature if we have received the Spirit of Christ and rejected the flesh. Peter and Jesus called it being born again. Anything else is carnal. I preach hard, the Spirit and mankind lives in two different worlds. Man must make some changes to cross over and can only do it with the help of the Spirit of God, if you find your life in this world, you have lost the Spirit of God, worth checking into. I'm sorry for people that have it so good in this world and bosting it to be the Spirit of God, NOT.

One needs to know the world he lives in and is aligned with. This world has a different spirit and is lost from the Spirit of God. I hope you have noticed, everything I have been writing is pointing to one thing, we must look to the Spirit of God in these last days. Every day, that gets more important from here on out.

I do not object to calling this whole Spiritual World, "An in-your-mind thing." I believe the Bible calls it the same thing. This is the reason we are told we can have the mind of Christ and many more such things. As I have said the mind and the spirit is the same organ in our body. Even the world has received this fact. Did you ever see the Paul Newman movie "Cool Hand Luke" where Paul Newman could not be shaped to fit in the old southern plantation prison? When the prison guards would punish him they would ask him, "You got your mind right, boy?" "You got your mind, right?"

I have used that story a few times in my forty years of preaching. When I started out preaching I got a few miles of revelations out of that line, "You got your mind right, boy?" God has told us to get our minds right, and Christians should never forget it. God cannot work with a cantankerous spirit, or mind. Even our head-shrinks speak of people with or without a right mind.

Head shrinks are trained to read and understand the spiritual side of man's mind. They don't like to call it that, it sounds too religious for them, implies a weakness below their education level they think. Our education is the most mind wrecking thing in this world. The mind is like everything else God created, it has two sides. The carnal side and the Spiritual side, the carnal side is evil and run by the spirits that were of the one third of God's created beings that rebelled from God and was threw out of heaven by Michael the Arc Angel. Ending up on the earth with mankind, God has had to restrain them ever since.

They are all carnal (Apart from God) and was totally defeated by Christ at the cross. They have been severely restricted since, they cannot lay a finger on me and you, except temping our minds with temptation of our own lust and ambitions of our own greedy bodies that are much carnal, and desire to run things over God. They will never do that. They have nothing but lies and lying promises for you and me to work with or against.

I have said and believe that anything, no matter how small, can infest and wreck one's entire mind if one allows it to do so. Satan is always trying to do that by setting on our carnal side and trying to kill the Spiritual side of our mind. He only must be allowed to possess it first, to completely control it. Satan is always trying to do just that. God has said he will turn a person over to a reprobate mind to believe a lie and be dammed, if that is what one desires. God gives us everything we desire and deserve.

God will not fight you, if he does, you are an instant looser. When Satan is controlling one's mind, he is in charge. This is what is known as, Devil possessed. I have stated, in my observations it seemed I could find more people possessed with religion, than perhaps any other subject. I would not know how to check it out for sure, just an opinion I guess.

A head-shrink is a trained expert in thinking he can handle the spirit side of mankind. The spirit like everything else, has distinctly two sides, good and evil If one does not know them apart, he could be a very dangerous man. Carnal man is always trying to operate on the spiritual side and does not know one thing about it. The man must know enough about the difference in the two worlds to be stable, God says a double minded man is unstable in all his ways. If one has not studied the Bible, he would not know much about a double mind.

Religion is a very powerful thing when it comes to handling mankind. The Devil is the most religious thing on earth. He will accept, claim and peddle, any false religion there is, like it will get you to heaven. He is not all that hard to please or get along with, just that you cannot get along well with anybody else. Have you ever been told, don't talk politics or religion to a friend? Ever wonder why? I've been told that, perhaps a few dozen times, but I still will not accept it.

A person that can't stand my religion is not my friend, and politics is not very far behind. That will solve that problem. You are free to check into it, a brother that places himself above or between me and my God cannot be my friend. How can Jesus stick closer to you than a brother when a brother insists on standing in between you and God? A many people cannot read their Bible very well and understands it less. And some of them are trying to preach, I pray for them, maybe God can use them some place. Hope their leading to, is greater than their leading away. God has told us to examine and judge ourselves.

I am no judge, but do know the Scriptures very well, and they will tell you about good and evil and am told the scriptures are Jesus Christ himself. He will be the judge, I would not want to get in his way. I hate to think of such a thing. I guess I missed a lot of things, but I was taught if one cannot say something to help a situation, it is probably better to just keep quite unless spoken to or asked something. We are told to pray without ceasing and preach the word to the world. He did not say, only if they like it or pay you well for it.

The Bible is Truth, truth is good, the world is carnal and is evil, evil is a lie. A man that preaches should know the difference. If he doesn't, how does he know what he is preaching? God says to establish every word from the mouth of two or three witnesses and the Bible being the only truth, I believe it would be the only place to find the witnesses that a child of God could depend on. God is always right, man is only right when he can be established in truth. We must not only know the truth, we are commanded to live and walk in Truth.

This is not as difficult as it sounds, one must believe and love God, put doubt from your mind he will do the rest. Satan and the world will break all contact with God for you, if you allow them to do it. The flesh must die out, it will lead into shipwreck, so we must meditate on God's Word day and night, resist the temptation of the flesh, putting it out of the mind. This can only be done if one will love and believe God and trust him. This is when the troublesome burdens and weights will leave one's body giving him the very energy to go on and be established in the right. I believe the word established is the key word in obtaining all these things, you can never do it trying to please both the world and God.

Satan is set with one-third of God's angels that rebelled for no other purpose than to knock you off your feet. Don't even think you can stand if you have not been established in the Spirit of God, which is the Word of God. Do not get confused in the switching around in so many names. Jesus, the Son of God, the Spirit of God, the Word of God, the Creator, and maybe a few dozen other names, are the same person. The Bible says so, and if you have one you have the others.

Satan is trying to separate them in anybody's mind that he can and confuse them with any way he can. Why we need to keep reading our Bible and not give any attention to Satan and his lies. Any time Satan is trying to give you an apple, you can bet it has a worm in it. We must learn the difference between the voice of God and the voice of Satan. If we don't we are living dangerously to say the least and time is getting shorter every day.

The difference in the voices are not so much in the tones of the voices, as in the contents of the message. *Mystery Babylon Whore* is coming up with this *Mark of the Beast* to install in a human body, to make it into a totally machine-controlled-beast. Neither one of these spiritual beast, are known to have the Spirit of Truth, or to tell anything but lies. If one will receive the Spirit of Jesus Christ which cannot receive any part of a lie and be led by it, this will be a guarantee that you will never be given this Mark of the Beast. This will separate the hypocrites and the ones who just think they have the Spirit. From the ones that are established in the Spirit of God. Though it may cost you your life if you have taken the Mark of the Beast.

I've often said there is a lot of people that just have enough religion to be miserable. I do not know where the cut off place is. I believe every man should have one. It should be at the place where it has been discovered. This, is why no man can ever judge another man. God has said for every man to judge himself. I know there is a place we can have enough to stand for ourselves and be sure of it. If you can believe God. God has assured us we will be a tried and proven people. There will be a record kept for the ones who failed, for there is no excuse for failing, for God will carry the ones through that cannot make it on their own. If they will just hold on to him.

It makes no difference if I judge you are not, you can be assured we will be judged by our creator. It is important to know the Word of God, and to have some close brethren that does, for we are told to look out for one another. Not to order one another around, but to preach and explain the Word. A person that hates to be corrected is more apt to be the one that is wrong. Instead of getting offended, one should learn to be able to explain himself and to convince the gainsayer. You will both learn to grow in the Lord by doing such.

I have been trying to bring this writing up and make a few points and drop a few facts that may be a little hard for some people to follow. Unless one can do a little research and studying. Any statement can be either proved or disapproved by the Bible if it concerns the Spirit or Life, if you will learn how to use it.

This is what will establish anyone with God and settle any disagreement between two level headed people. That rest entirely upon the individual, just how much he can receive, explain and believe the Bible. I maintain that I can establish, any quote in here that I have made, by two or three witnesses from the Bible. Or I will do some heavy apologizing, and some thanking somebody that will show me my mistake.

I just want it to come from the Bible, it has already judged everything. It is the only thing I know that is always right, and the only thing God will need to use at judgment. We all have more to be thankful for than we like to admit. One can find that out if he will study the Bible. It is the Language of the Spirit of God, it is

Jesus in person. It is the Bible, the King James. The one and only thing that is nothing but truth, and the whole Truth.

God has said, he will put it in the hearts of the antichrist kingdoms to hate the Mystery Babylon Whore. They are to eat her flesh and burn her with fire from the earth. This is not hard to see coming and why. The Antichrist Muslims are built on hating and sworn to kill all Christians from the earth. While the Mystery Babylon Whore will accept any religion on the earth, that will accept the Pope as God. They are trying to get together now, and we know they are going to make it, for a short while, God says they will.

How do they think they are going to get them two religions together? No ship has been sent to sail with two captains, at least and came back that way. The Antichrist will war with and defeat the False Prophet, as God wrote. Together they will go after the annihilation of the Jews. You can tell any false religion, it will always hate the Jews. That will place them against Jesus Christ and will bring about their end. Jesus casting them into the lake of fire that burns forever and ever. The Devil will be locked up with a seal of darkness, and put into the pit, for a thousand years. Jesus, will be ruling the world without the Devil being there to temp them.

You can read all about it in the Bible. Talk about a good book?! I do not believe it has an equal, one of a kind. The record of the world and all humankind from the beginning of man to the end of man. Covering everything in between that pertains to mankind's future including where one will spend eternity. No excuse for one to miss heaven, if he can read his Bible, and believe God.

3

"A FEW WORDS ABOUT RELIGION"

RELIGION, MAY BE THE most powerful thing to man on the earth, every man has his own. Has been that way since creation when God gave man the garden. I have written much on how God has made most everything in twos, religion is no different. There is the true religion, which is the Spirit of Christ, the Truth. And there is the Antichrist religion which is nothing but Satan and a lie from the ground up. But Satan will buy and peddle any and every false religion that comes by, that is his business. True and false have been battling each other since the creation, probably before, and will be battling one another every day as long, as time, as we know it, does exist.

The Bible has recorded the history of man, from the beginning in the garden, to the last day that time will exist. We can read all about it in the Bible, seems kind of amazing to me. For there is not a false statement in it, nor a word left out of it, even though we will not fully understand it without help from the Spirit of God. The Bible says so. The Bible is the Spirit of God and record of man from the beginning to the end but says very little about God himself before or after mankind, it would have very little to do with our salvation. But promises no word in it will fail until all be fulfilled. There is where faith must come in.

When you are reading the Bible, you are reading God's judgement on everything. Dealt to every person the same way. I have written in other books, and maybe this one, about how everything is what it is, depending on where one is looking at it from. And how the Spirit and the carnal are looking at everything from the opposite side from one another. They just about see nothing alike, why we must always look at things from God's point of view.

The Spirit of God is always seeing things correctly. The Spirit of God should be in everybody while bringing them all together in one, for the betterment of every person. Together we can pull a big load easier. Pulling against each other, we can move nothing. It would be a glorious sight if we could all hear and believe everything in Truth, which is Jesus Christ. The world could not withstand us. God is the Truth, anything contrary to him is carnal and a lie, and will never make it into the Spirit of God. This can only be seen and done, in and by, the Spirit, which is The Word of God.

I know this is hard for a carnal man to appreciate and I can tell you why. Man is very likely to ask, "What's in this for me?" when he has been offered any deal. The Bible is about nothing for sale but a secure future in the hereafter promised all through the Word of God and does not promise anything "To me" past eternal life with Christ.

Mankind is so selfish and carnal, he cannot completely fit with another man, only in the Spirit. This leaves out all mankind if his flesh cannot die out. How many men do you know that is agreeable to that? I am me, and you are you, we can become one only in the Spirit, it is the only thing that can tolerate us both.

Religion, is simply what a person believes in and what he looks towards to put his trust into for eternity, two choices. It might not be so important if it was not so permanent, like forever. But it is, the most permanent thing you will ever face in this life. We go through life making choices, every choice we make, we will live or die with it.

God says we will give account for every idle word. This does not necessarily mean one will be judged for every word one utters, but we will be accountable for every word one says by the way we said it, for the rest of our life, if he does not repent. This is the reason we must be going through life repenting for we would never make it otherwise. Repentance comes from the heart, God looks nowhere else for it. He knows the very thoughts and intents of the heart of everyone. Can you explain that to a carnal mind? A carnal mind cannot reach around it. Ever hear anyone ask, got your mind right, boy? We can have the mind of Christ.

We serve God by faith, faith is believing. A carnal man cannot believe it, so he cannot have it. Sounds to me like that kind-of leaves the carnal man out. When I came to be reading these things in the Bible, I got interested in checking out a little bit of what God considers carnal to be. I consulted my dictionary to see what it said, it said no more or less than this, carnal is, "Anything apart from the Spirit." No wonder God talked so much about it. I hardly know of any plainer or bigger word than that. It kind of underlined all my preaching of how important the Spirit is, and how needful it is to get to knowing something about it. God is The Spirit, anything apart from him is carnal and dead.

Then comes the importance of how lost and helpless we are without the Spirit. Enough to get a sober man to thinking. God said to establish every word with two or three witnesses. I have figured out that is talking about both ends of the word. Where it came from and where it is going, by the way it is used. If one becomes that well informed I promise one will have fewer discussions about the Bible and less people trying to instruct him. They will more than apt want to hear from him. If they care about their soul. Some just do not believe and rather not hear you talk about it. That is one of each man's choices and all men's problem, he will live and die with his choices.

Now, I do not know in every case if that is good or bad, but know it is an automatically sure thing. People have a dread and sometimes a dislike for the plain truth, when they have been feeding on a lie and their flesh enjoying it. The Bible will expose and condemn all lies if you can quote and establish the Bible correctly. These things underline my, kind-of, dislike for denominations. I know their answers for being wrong, "Oh but nobody can be perfect all the time."

Jesus Christ, was and is, the Bible is perfect and says so. If the person is trying to cut me down and put me in my place or justify himself, he is very wrong, for I am not talking about me, but the Bible and Truth. It is not wrong, nowhere in it. If I am misquoting it, that is another horse and of a different color. But like I was saying there is a way of establishing every word with the Bible, or God would not have told us to do it. But he did and told us how. How many people do you see that knows that? Or better yet, how many do you see that does it?

Jesus Christ is truth, no part of a lie in him, carnal is nothing but a lie. True religion is nothing but truth and God's Word. So, true religion will accept no part of a lie but only truth, while carnal accepts any religion on the earth but truth, telling all people it will save their soul while promising them everything they want here and in the hereafter. Where is Satan going to come up with life and heaven for all his people on this earth?

He was cast out of heaven; his lies are innumerable and sound so good the world wants to believe them, and the world can do as it pleases. Adam and Eve gave the world to Satan. Every person either believes and is led by the Spirit of God or he belongs to Satan. I cannot change that story.

I do not want seventy-two virgins and all the dope in the world when I get to heaven. Any man that will fall for that does not have a sound mind and he will never find such a heaven as that. With Jesus Christ, I do not plan to be apart from the Spirit. Jesus is the Spirit and our only hope on this earth. That will not bring you many compliments, so my writings will not impress the world.

John said, if every word was written that should be written about Jesus Christ, he reckoned the books of the world could not contain them. I fully believe there is not a wrong word, over exaggerated word, or one word used in the Bible that is not supposed to be in the Bible. That means I believe every word that is written in the King James Authorized Translation. Jesus said he wrote it, and it is him. We are told to preach it to every creature in the earth. That includes every word that is in it now, and forever. God never changes. Are you looking for a writer that can offer you more, I am not he?

If man adds or changes one word in it, it cannot Spiritually, or legally, be called the King James Authorized Bible. The Bibles that have been changed and rewritten must be labeled by the name of the ones that wrote them or at least authorized them. They will be responsible for their work. It will be counted among the books of the world, even if some of them are mighty good books. Jesus did not write them, or at least did not say he did. He claims the original King James and tells when, where, how and why, he did it, around sixteen-hundred AD. In all other writings, that is, or has been, I have not read where Jesus claimed writing a word of them. The Bible is the only Spiritually written book on this earth.

I have not even heard of a book or any writings that can even start to equal or claim the honorary standings or credits that is accredited to the King James Translated Bible. It stands in an honor all by itself. Several millions of people have died protecting it from Satan's false religions in the world in just these last one thousand years, it has been written by King James' Authorization. The Devil has hated it more than Jesus Christ himself. He thought he killed Jesus. But he just woke up his influence, he lost that battle very greatly. A testament is not sealed until the testator is dead.

I am forced to believe that all other writings in the world must be called carnal writings, while the entire King James contains, only and all, the Spiritual Writings that is on, or has been on, this earth. Not all the writings about the Spirit, but all the writings of the Spirit. I do not know of another power that can touch its shadow or can even get close enough to see it. It takes the Spirit of God.

This should give any Christian a window to see why the Bible, is and should be, such a cherished and

Holy Book. Jesus said, it was the Way, the Truth, the Life, the Light, the Spirit, and everything else that is right and positive. Even said it was him. One can only see that with the Spirit of God, and some of our largest denominations does not even believe in the Spirit of God. What do they believe in beside what they already have? Who is going to resurrect them, their father? Here on the Earth? They sure do not have a computer that can resurrect anybody. If someone in the world is trying to reason a rewritten Bible and a corrected one to you, ask him when did Jesus tell anyone he was going to need himself corrected, or updated? He *is* the Spirit, he can start in where the computer leaves off.

What I am trying to say is, every word that is in the King James Bible is a Spiritual Word. It has the power of the Spirit with it, when used properly. Any word that is not in the King James Bible is a carnal word and will need to be able to be established by two and three places in the Bible as to how it is used, or it cannot be considered as a Gospel Word.

I am not really moved by a carnally preached sermon. I will try to get as much out of it as I can but will be measuring every word of it from the Bible, it is the judge, it has already judged the world and everything in it. When you read it, you are reading God's judgment on anything it is about, for it is what God is going to use on Judgment day. It will not have one word changed in it, what it means today is what it will mean on judgment day. What it will mean on judgment day is what it means today. Why argue about the scriptures, just establish each word as God commanded us to do and accept it? No person is anointed above you other than to preach the gospel, it is up to you to receive it for yourself, not him to force feed you.

Too many people want to hold onto the world with one hand and the Lord with the other. I do not know if they will make it or not, but I do know if one knows God, he will be one miserable person until he gets it right with God or at least thinks he has. And will seldom be a person that lives to be an old man if he chooses to live his life battling with the Spirit of the Lord. It is always right and not known for giving much quarters to anything that is wrong. Wrong is out of God's territory. We are to seek God, not command or instruct him.

You ask him about things, you don't tell him anything. There is nothing he don't know. If his chosen cannot take orders, they will not be given any from God. Satan has a lot of people thinking they are in charge, but they are only in charge of the Devil's people not of them that are of God. You can take that to the bank, if you are not bankrupted, they will cash it for you.

I am hoping to build this writing up to a few points, or facts, that I can drop and will be understood to the reader as I am meaning to use them. I am fully convinced that any word you can find in the Bible is a Spiritual Word. Any word you cannot find in the Bible is a carnal word. Since God confused the one whole language that the earth used, to divide up the people at the tower of Babel, an ordinary man knew not one word of Spiritual Language and had very little of God in him but the fear. Until Jesus came. Maybe Daniel, Elijah, Solomon and a very few others, but I hardly call them ordinary men. The world had Moses and the prophets.

Jesus the Spirit, was not given to man until around the year of 00 on our calendar. I do not know a person who knows exactly when that was except on the calendar. I have never saw it there. God spoke in his book to the Hebrews, "God, who at sundry times and in diver's manners spoke in time past unto the fathers by the prophets, hath in these last days spoken unto us by his Son." This is where the New Testament comes in.

Until Jesus came and paid the price for mankind and sent back the Spirit of God unto all mankind, we had very little of anything of God except his word, spoken through his prophets, kings, and judges. Jesus Christ had not been given to man. If you will look very close at the Bible and history, man had a deep inborn fear of God, that he does not have today, he blasphemes, mocks, and laughs at God with no fear at all. God did not put up with that before Christ came.

God said them that have no God at all, will think more of their god than the ones that have a living God that loves them. God did not put up with any of that before Jesus became the mediator between man and God, the prophets, could not do it. Man would not accept another man, and no man could live long enough to carry it on. God is love and them that know him loves his Son, them that know Jesus loves and trust God. They come together. There are not words to make us understand how much Jesus paid for God's Word to stay alive until he got his harvest picked from this world.

Jesus gave us so much, and it seems instead of us giving him the love and thanks he deserves, we are giving him ridicule and mockery. It will get worse and worse until Jesus will be forced to burn clean, all the evidence of all mankind that would not receive him, that ever existed. Leaving only the smoke of their torment and keeping the few that he accepted for the Father. I know of no one that knows what the smoke will look like. Maybe it will be a little coloration around a small spot like a cloud, just a guess. The clouds are out there in the atmosphere all time if you are seeing them or not. I am sure it will look like torment.

As I wrote in one of my other books, "God will have the last laugh." God has mentioned in his Word, he will laugh at the foolishness of man. He has told us to wise-up, and how to do it, no need for man to stay that way. It is his choice.

I cannot say any more than the Word of God says about this, but I know most people have a question in their mind about the burning up the earth and all the elements thereof. But before I make another comment on anything, I want you to know God can do anything he pleases and any way he chooses. He is going to do everything he says he is going to do. He doesn't need to have my opinion on anything. There is a lot of room for God to operate in when it comes to making everything new. Like he said he was going to do.

When I was born again I was made into a new creature, but I look entirely like the same body to the carnal. When God makes all things new when he returns, like he promised just as he was leaving, all carnal will be gone. I am not going to argue with him about one thing, it will be alright with me, I promise you. Do you think you can trust your neighbor to make all things new, rather than the creator? I believe I rather stay with Jesus he is the only sure thing. He is the Truth; the most powerful thing God has put here on the earth. He is God, the fullness of him, the greatest thing that has ever been given to the earth. He is called the Savior of mankind. If anyone is dissatisfied with this world and life, he needs to get to know him. He is a Spirit and the only way out of this world, anything else you will be locked into it for eternity. Don't even think God has not warned us, he died for us.

4

IN THE BEGINNING

THIS WORLD HAS ONE big problem that started when God created Eve and gave her to Adam. Obviously, she was meant to be under subjection to Adam, as the lesser half. I know that the women do not want to acknowledge any of that, but I am only lead by God's Word, and anybody that can read it and not see that, is throwing God out of his own picture. That comes with the "Mark of the Beast."

Your part in it is nothing to me, except, I have been told to preach it to the world that will hear, they will just have to take the remainder up with God. I only preach his Word, I am not a judge or an enforcer of it. I do not read where God called any such person to work in his kingdom, and I am not the Pope. Adam named the woman the mother of all living. Mother is a big word, used in a lot of ways, but boils down to about the same thing, any place it is applied. I read no place where woman has been given authority over the man. But, several places where one took it and there was usually chaos. Makes for some of the biggest stories in the Bible.

The story of Adam and Eve and the snake didn't make a very big rail, in the spirit world, just the beginning of our world. But amplifies all the happenings of the carnal world. I can start any place in history and tell you any story ever told, or written, and Identify the same three spirits of Adam and Eve and the snake. People that do not know the spirit of what they are dealing with, and the spirit that they are dealing from, are deaf, blind, and know nothing in the real world, Jesus says. And at the end of man's allotted time he will pass on, with nothing to show for it. Only what he has gained carnally, and he cannot take that with him, not one thing. I heard a preacher say once that he had several times saw a lot of people following a Hearst to the graveyard to put someone away. But had never seen one with a U-Haul trailer behind it. Made a point I guess.

The carnal (Apart from the Spirit) is just a reflection of the real thing, the Spirit is the real thing. If you know the spirit of something, you can very well read it off. Spirits stay very close to their source, or purpose. Jesus says the spirit is the life of anything that has life in it. When the spirit, or ghost, leaves something, it is dead. The dictionary, says carnal is anything apart from the Spirit. God says anything carnal is dead.

The snake used a lie and deceit to temp Eve, Eve used the same thing to temp Adam, I guess Satan, as usual, sat back and laughed, and had nothing involved except his mouth. God got him anyway. Every story in the Bible, one can usually come up with an instigator (Lie), a tail bearer (Deceit), and an intended (Victim). For everything has already been judged, just read it in the Word of Truth, the only thing that will set anybody free is the truth. The truth is Jesus Christ, and I see no place in his word where he put man under subjection of the woman, in naming their duties or positions, or authority. There is no way to get quicker or farther away from God than telling a Lie. God hates them all, if it is contrary to the Word of God, it is a lie. Or to say it is God's Word when it is not, is another lie. God has told us to be careful and slow about what we say. To purposely misrepresent something for what it is not is a lie and may be the most commonly used lie in the books. It is very damming for anybody.

When Bill Clinton raised the turn for the governor of Arkansas from two to four years. Clinton promised us, if we would reelect him to the four-year turn, he would serve it out, and do certain things and not run for president in the next two years. I did not vote for him, I had already learned, you could not depend on anything he said. I grew up being taught and believing, if a man's word was no good, then he was no good. I will die believing it, I've seen it proved over and over. Show me a politician that will keep his word and not lie, and I will show you a *rare as hen's teeth*, thing.

As soon as Bill got the election, he started his campaign for the president's seat in the White House. That he had been running for since he was born. Telling his left headed liberal bunch, including the news media, to get out there and Attack! Attack! Attack, was his very words. Democrats have used that slogan ever since. A few lies and an attack, attack, attack. When you got something that works, wear it out, I guess. Satan believes in that. Bill and Hillary may have been two of the best Democrats every. They sure ranked high on my list of liars.

They have fully convinced me that anybody that is a good enough liar can become president, but that don't make him to be a good person. Obama should have convinced everybody of that. You can measure a lot of a country by the leaders they elect for themselves like America does. If somebody wants to correct me, just explain why this country is twenty trillion dollars under water. I might listen to him a little. We used to be wealthy and prosperous, but now we are among the most indebted nations in the world, and maybe the least feared and respected. I believe we need to set in a new bunch of rulers. United in the Lord Jesus Christ. When we were there, no other nation could touch us. The world set in to make us ashamed that we were exceptional. God said he would make the world envious of his chosen people because of their prosperity, what is that to be ashamed of? We do not have to be ashamed of it now, for we have lost it some time ago.

I well know, that no one president made all that debt. But Obama, very plainly put us under double the amount that every president before him had done, put together. Of course, Obama hated us as well as the whole Left does. I do not know why the few that are left that loves and appreciates America cannot see that, blind like God says, I guess.

I have been trying to shed a little light on how low this country is sinking. It is like looking down into a drilled well, I don't have a light to shine that low, to the bottom. Especially, when I get my head beside it to try and see. But I can hear what is going on down there, and the Bible has already warned us about every bit of it. But, one must study the Bible to see it coming and without God's Spirit you cannot see it, sometimes even after it is here. When man don't shoulder the responsibility that God laid out for him, he is as worthless as one dirty sock, with a hole in it. How many banks do you know will just keep making loans when there is no collateral or payback? How long would that bank last? Do you think God is not as smart as a banker?

Them that think that Obama was so good for us; give me ten trillion dollars plus eight years of taxes this country pays in to spend in eight years and I believe I could give us a better time of eight years than he did. Would that make me a hero and highly intelligent in so many people's book keeping? No, not unless they could become rich with it. I believe I could give them back a little change. Obama did not, if he had any change left he put it into his pocket with the rest of it. God says the love of money is the root of all evil.

I do not see that Obama might be the smartest man in the world. But I guess I cannot rate smart men very well, like Democrats can, it is for sure they don't think I can. I am not writing this book to try to win any favoritism. But I am very interested in the very soul of our great country. I have a book published, "Our Great Country America is Dying." On sail where books are sold.

I am convinced that no one can save it but the people in it. If they loved it like God does, it should not be any problem. It just seems to me that mankind is just too much in love with himself to care about anyone else or a country. That fellow is no good for anybody but himself and he is self's worst enemy. The world cannot be nothing but misery to such a person. This, is why our nation is going down for sure.

I fail to see why the world or any country in it, cannot pick up a true history book and see how England was given the Bible, held it high in front of them and very quickly became the most powerful nation on the earth, with the most powerful and feared navy and army that had ever been on the earth. Until Mystery Babylon took it over and set the government into setting in God's seat and running the church and ran the pilgrims and puritans out of the country. They came to America but brought the Bible with them. A lot of history, but in a short time in comparison God grew American up into the greatest nation on the earth. Defeated England and won two world wars with everybody else that crossed them and their God.

The rest of the world sees where our power is at and hates the God of our Bible with an unto-death passion. Over half of the people in America today have joined Mystery Babylon and want to help our enemies tear America into oblivion, any way they can. Can somebody explain that to me? I myself, can see nothing past Devil Possessed.

God is the protector of nations, any nation that does not know God is being run by Satan and can expect anything. I guess God should have let Japan drop the Bomb on us. He very well could have, you know. We had a little Godliness left in us at that time, but now I'm not so sure. It is for sure the only thing that will keep our heads above water. I am tired of supporting our Babylon Schools, they are at the very foundation of this nation's problems. They have us completely on the verge of another Civil War, they started the other one, and I believe they have an intention to start this one. The left has completely accepted the Muslim Religion and outlawed ours. There is no better description for a Democrat than that.

5

"GLENN BECK'S STORY"

GLENN BECK HAS BEEN talking about some of the same things, that I started this book about. Although he never brought the Bible, or Spirit of God into it, or made any connection to them. I don't know why; his story was so much the same thing I've been studying and writing about. I was sore amazed at just how far out and clear the Bible explains it. The most amazing thing to me was how close the scientist was saying it was to being upon us. I hope they are wrong, but they are our most educated people we have.

His story was about a certain two scientists. He spent some time telling about how renowned they both were, and how reliable they both were in their work.

One was working on making and developing a computerized man in these fleshly bodies, with actual ability to produce and maintain its own intelligence and making its own decisions, having its own computer mind. They said it had the potential, almost for sure, that it would make a normal man obsolete. One was heading this project, the other was very much involved and aware of everything and was just as confident and as assuring as the first one. Saying they were so close upon it they would have it ready to turn out in four years, it would be the end of all flesh. This is year 2017, four more years would put time into 2021.

The other was working on going to Mars to set up a place for mankind to have a new territory on Mars to colonize some of the people, so man would not become extent. They were, in agreement that man as we know him was going to be gone if they didn't find him a place to set himself up to recolonize himself. Used the expression one time that it would be "The end of all flesh." Jesus used that same expression, when he talked of his coming back to save the Jews.

They claimed he would be on Mars with his project in ten more years. They did not say if this man-made man could reproduce itself or not but was referring to it like it could. I do not know. Keep in mind, Satan is a copier, he cannot create anything.

This was about the first time I heard of AI (Artificial Intelligence) which has become a household word since.

Normally, I would have laughed at such news. But I was already into studying and making notes on "The Mark of the Beast," to write this book that I felt like

God was telling me to write. As a matter of fact, I had already started the book.

As I listened to Glenn, I was almost floored, I never heard him come up with one line that I could not have told him, "That sounds just like the same thing I've been reading about and just the way Jesus told it." But it is not going to be this second scientist saving all flesh on Mars, it is going to be Jesus Christ's second coming back for his that did not take the "Mark of a Man, or Beast." In their forehead, or in their hands, or the number of the beast, which is the number 6.6.6 + just as far as you want to run them out or stack them up.

Now I am not referring to these scientist in any singular form, I have no idea of how many are in their organization or how much tax money they are given for their projects. I would assume a plenty, since government is not subjected to any natural laws. This, is why, it hates the Bible, and determined to kill it, any way they possibly can. It is like a finger in their eye. How long do you think they can operate above it when there are no such thing as free meals, somebody pays for them?

Six, six, six is the number of a man, times man, times man. The number seven is God's number and man will never reach it without the Spirit of God, always one short. No matter how many men they multiply and stack up, they cannot reach the Spiritual world from the carnal world. Truth is between them. This is well spoken in the Bible. Jesus left this world saying he was going to prepare us a place and bring it back to us,

and it will not be on Mars. Said if he did not, there
would be *no flesh left*. It will be all spiritual with God
setting in it, after he has destroyed and burned up this
entire creation and every soul that doesn't love Truth.
After Jesus destroys all the flesh left on the earth in the
great Battle of God Almighty, called it in the Hebrew
tongue, Armageddon. And the new heaven and Earth
will come down. Read all about it in the Bible. In the
book of Revelations, John saw it, and was told to write
it down.

I know where the ones are coming from to take the
"Mark of the Beast" they think they are going to break
the bands that Jesus Christ has on carnal man. Even the
sentence of death on all or any carnality.

A computer can throw thousands of facts together
at one time and give you the sum, or the answer almost
instantly. How many times better is that than a fleshly
brain that can hardly figure two things at a time? But
the computer will never take God's place, maybe man's,
but not God's.

These scientists assured us they were almost there,
and their robot-humans would work efficiently and
effectively. Satan will convince the people they can
kill Christ. In time this will bring on the Battle of
Armageddon, (In the hills around Jerusalem). This
has been Satan's dream and purpose since the battle in
heaven and Lucifer was cast out. Mankind fell to the
same place as Satan when he failed and was cast out
from God. I was literally amazed, you would think they
were getting the whole Idea from Jesus Christ himself,

but they did not include the Spirit of God or Bible, not even in one line. It seems no carnal humans ever do, not even our preachers most of the time, our school teachers would be thrown into jail if they did. Satan does not want Christ mixed into any teaching to our children. That is what some of my writing was intended to be about. When you are a believer, you must include God in everything. Jesus said we can do nothing without him, and nothing against truth, only for it.

You listen to any report, or any discussion of any problem, or something gone wrong, Jesus is their answer if they could just see it. But they cannot seem to think of him, or put their trust in him, only to blame him. Carnal can never succeed in doing that. Only in the mind of Satan's people.

I will give you an example: When the first big school shooting happened, in Columbine, Colorado. People were shocked, even though David Wilkerson had been telling us for around three years it was coming.

When it happened, for the next few weeks you could hear or see on the TV everywhere, the experts discussing what could have cause such a thing and wanting to come up with something they could do to make sure it never happened again. It seemed to me I listened to about everything that could be thought of by man. No telling how much tax money was paid to influential men and college professors to give their opinions. But not one person did I hear bring up the subject of teaching and training our children in the fear and admonition of the Lord, like my Bible said for us to do. They will never solve the problem any other way. How can one get them to see that? God says they are blind.

Of course, that was in a time you could be thrown into jail if you mentioned the name of Jesus Christ or carried a Bible into a schoolhouse in front of an atheist's kid. His religion, like a Muslim's, has the full constitutional protection, while it gives Christian a jail sentence for *thinking* a silent prayer to Jesus Christ on government property. The Democrats were running the government.

Some was calling it the "think law," —Christians think that is a great law. I do not see how a person in his right mind would call that law Good or helpful. At least they were acting like it, they voted for Obama anyway, two times. Satan has gotten the minds of most of the people gone completely off their rail. The Jesus hating, Devil possessed, left headed Democrats was in control of all of Washington DC. With the full intention of dividing our country again. And was throwing Chaplains out of the services for the mention of Jesus while in uniform. Spineless Republicans with weak knees were helping them, afraid they would get threw out of Washington DC like Newt Gingrich, and Bob Barr did. I guess Christians were hiding under the table if there were any Christians. If you would have told me, thirty years ago, that these things would be happening in America today, I would have told you, you were crazy. I thought this country had more sense than that. But it has happened.

I told everybody that would listen, especially my kids, and grandkids, church and neighbors. That if the two shooters had been brought up in a Christian home and *trained* in the fear and admonition of the Lord, you could not have paid them enough to carry a loaded rifle into that school house. That is the difference the engrafted Word of God would make. Democrats think it is the gun's fault, outlaw the gun and it will end all problems. How stupid can one people get? They only desire to make the people helpless to ever rise against the government run by Satan, even for their own survival. They demand to be in total control of our thinking, as our God.

When government is your God, you better get along with him. You look over the people in the world today, I could be convinced they are raving mad. All of them cannot be that stupid. There must be another reason, wanting attention perhaps, and wanting to feel like they can speak with authority. Being able to criticize God and convince people around you, will accomplish both. Many, other reasons I could think of, for sure. Mainly God has turned them over to a reprobate mind to believe a lie that they might be dammed, read about it in Romans: One. God will not play around with anybody. Look what happens every time he gives man a little slack.

I know how difficult it is to get out of school disagreeing with them. I almost didn't get through high school. It took me three schools and two years to get through the twelfth grade. It was not because I could not learn, I just could not agree with a lot of things they started teaching in the early nineteen-fifty's. Like there is no such thing as absolutes, (Meaning no God) and the earth was maybe fifty thousand years old instead of six like we had always been told, and a person could be any sex that he wanted to be. People evolved from monkeys. There was no such thing as the earthly flood told about in the Bible, when there is a mountain of evidence on every continent. Several other things that they have not made me believe yet. I was telling them then they were crazy, and still telling them today. But you cannot tell a reprobate minded person about truth, he cannot hear it.

With the False Prophet Doctrine coming from the False Prophet there in Rome, naming the curriculum in our schools, and outlawing our Bibles. One of the Three Great Evil Spirits that John saw coming out of the mouth of the dragon, the mouth of the beast, the mouth of the False Prophet, sent to go forth to the kings of the earth working lying miracles to gather them to the battle of that great day of God Almighty. At a place called in the Hebrew Tongue Armageddon. Told about there in the sixteenth chapter of Revelations when the sixth angel poured out his vial upon the river Euphrates. To make a way for the kings of the east to come into Europe. That is so plain a blind man can see it.

Out of all the unbelievable things that man has come up with, like carrying a TV around in your watch pocket; talking, sending, and receiving messages all over the globe being covered with satellites, I could list a few dozen more things.

To let Holly Wood and the left headed liberal Democrats, outlaw Christianity in our country, and let our President announce to us this is a Muslim nation now and not a Christian nation anymore. Is among the most unbelievable things I believe I've seen in my seventy-eight years of this country. What has happened to the Americans that I grew up with? I say the world has gone Devil possessed and seems to be crazy proud of it.

What is it that Paul and Peter wrote so much about that men despised so badly? Everybody seems to be seeking after, for themselves. It is "Authority," I wrote in some of my other books, it may be one of the most sought-after things on this Earth, authority. Mankind despises any authority that does not belong to himself.

By taking the "Mark of the Beast" they think they have broken the authority of Jesus over them, for that is what the Antichrist and scientist are teaching them, and our children. They will get them to join them to try and kill Christ at the battle of Armageddon, the largest army ever formed on the Earth. God teaches, that has been the soul dream and purpose for Satan since the creation. We have given them our children to raise as they please. Takes a load off our responsibility, don't you agree? If Americans are sunk that low as to refuse responsibility for their children, it sounds to me like goodbye to America and our children.

Listen to the God haters, the ones in Holly Wood, the ones on television, the ones in politics, our teachers in colleges, how ungodly they love to talk! And think they are so brave and smart, as to be an adviser to God that created us all. When they do not know him. I believe we should be trying to get our country and children back from the Mystery Babylon Whore before it is too late. She surely has taken them. I have written a book on that. Titled; "Mystery Babylon Revealed." One can be ordered where books are sold.

The ones that has taken the "Mark of the Beast" might as well go with Satan for it will be too late for them, unless they are willing to turn against the Devil and be killed for it, is the way I read it. These are the ones that will be running to the mountains and praying for the rocks to fall on them, to hid them from the one that is setting on the throne. But death will flee from them, for Jesus has said if they take the Mark, they will drink of his wrath and blood, for five months.

Over one hundred-pound balls of hail falling on them, midst fire and blood, the sun scorching them that are refusing him. Locus scorpions the shape of horses, stinging them with their tails hanging off them with heads on the ends of their tails like a snake's head. They bite and sting like a scorpion, Jesus says. The world given blood to drink instead of water. Many men being killed. Is just a few of the things happening to them when God pleads with them by pouring out his wrath, on the world. I am not telling it one bit worse than it is told in the Bible it is going to be. I do not believe one can tell it that bad.

I do not believe in a rapture like the big boys preach, because I simply cannot find it in my Bible. It cannot be established from the Bible without adding many words to God's word, and he has said to not do that. But just lately I do believe that God is not going to let his saved children go through the full wrath of God. It will not be hard for God to protect them, for they will all be gathered with him there near Jerusalem. I do not find where there is going to be a handful of Christians left living on earth, when he pours out his wrath. I cannot find very many of them right now. We have not entered his wrath yet. We still have a long way to go, and it is going to get rougher every day. I doubt if anyone living today will see any of the worst.

You would have thought by the way the scientist was telling about the people perishing, they were telling it from the Bible, but I do not believe a carnal human can read the Bible and understand any word coming from the Spirit of God. Least, it says they cannot without help from someone or something coming from God.

As I have already said, I have never found where Jesus has lied to us yet. After forty years of teaching and preaching and five years of writing, I can see many things that I used to not be able to see, and many more new things happening seems like every day. Like Jesus becoming the one Spiritual Language to put us all back together again as they were when they started building the tower at Babel. I am trying to put some of these into my writings to where a common man can understand, if he will open his eyes and look over the world a little. I think he can believe it. God has showed me so much, it is hard for me to put it all together, with so little education, but I do not know a school where I could receive this kind of so called education.

So, I'll be bouncing around a lot, but will always try to come back to the subject. If you will try to stay with me, I will try to finish my stories to some satisfaction. I promise they will be established by the Bible, being my intention. In reading about the way people will be acting; cursing God; blaming him; instead of repenting. I've always wondered how the Devil could get such a hold on mankind to keep them from turning to God and refusing to quit worshiping material things made by man's hands instead of God. He only has access to one side of our mind.

I've been watching our politicians, our world leaders, and the things man is doing, and the things he has built, these past forty years or more, absolutely, unbelievable. And now they are going to change mankind into being run by a computer, the ones that will receive the "Mark of the Beast." At the tower of Babel, Jesus said if he didn't confuse them and divide them, they were coming together as one against God and nothing would be restrained unto them. So, he pulled our one language from the earth, that the whole earth spoke when man started to build the tower at Babel. He scattered the people to slow them down and they have been scattered since. Jesus would like to see that same ego again, but this time *with* God, not contrary to him.

I am still a bunch confused even if he has written it down here in the Bible for us to read. But I am about convinced, that there is nothing that man will not try to do. And will bow to nothing but force, lust, lies, and self-glory. A man that has been turned over to a reprobate mind loves a lie and seems to be unable to believe the truth. Would not that be the definition of a reprobate mind? One that has been turned over to a computer control? God has sent him strong delusions to believe a lie and be dammed. Read about it in Romans one. God says with him nothing is impossible.

Did you ever wonder why a man as merciful as Jesus who loved us enough to give himself as a sacrifice to save us? Even after the shameful way mankind, unmercifully treated him, and killed him. It appears that Jesus was the one that did not know what they were doing. But I am sure he did. The big question is, why?

Well, he told us why, if one will read his word he gave to us, with any understanding. I believe the big word would be because he *loved* us so. Again, he is also a God of judgement, and is going to judge all of mankind, one at a time. He has plainly told us that our flesh has completely fell from God and is destined to die and perish. But our spirit and soul can be saved. He will not use force, any religion that thinks they can use force for converts like Mystery Babylon and Islam. Is not of Jesus Christ, you can rest assured.

The "Mark of the Beast" will seal the fate of them that take it unless they sacrifice their own bodies to save themselves and come into the Spirit of God, is the way it sounds to me. When God told me to write a book, he said he was going to keep me going until I got it wrote, unless I gave up on writing it. After five years, he has convinced me that he meant what he said. Now, I could write another book on how he did that, but no, thank you. I'm still trying to finish this one.

Thanks to Glenn Beck, I believe I have come up with the end for it. If I can just get it to *"gather."* When Beck told of what them scientist were coming up with, like a computerized human, completely controlled by a computer, and they had it about ready to turn out. Made me feel better about myself, if a man with Glenn Beck's intelligence, and standing, would buy it, maybe I was not completely crazy after all. It gave me some hope, he explained to me what God was telling me. Jesus knew all about it two thousand years ago.

When Lucifer rebelled from God, he swore he'd set his seat in the north parts above God's and receive the worship of the congregation. With God, worship, consists of giving honor and glory to something. God has said we are to give him the honor and Glory in everything. If one does not give God the Glory in anything, he does not have the glory to give to the one. We must give God all the honor and glory in everything first. If we don't, we give it all to Satan. All, that does not go to God, the Devil receives, says the Bible.

When one is giving his body to serve the Devil, he is robing God of his glory that belongs to him and giving glory to Satan. That man will not be honored by God but destroyed with the Devil. God is a jealous God. God has already judged just that. God has said, in the last days, the world will take after the Antichrist. I have already written much about how it will come down to where one will have to make a choice between the two. Taking the "Mark of the Beast" or "Jesus Christ" is the big choice we will have to decide.

I believe we, with any Bible teaching and living in America, had better learn to appreciate it, and start to protect the rights we have left before it is too late. I have always said, Americans will be the most excuseless people to ever stand in front of God. The Antichrist with his God haters are raising up in a mighty fast and powerful way. I am trying as hard as I can to wake a few of us up. I have spent what little life savings I had in the past five years, getting these books printed and published. I would recommend to anybody that is raising kids, or planning on living a few more years, to very seriously read some in them. I hope I am improving with my writing ability, It can sure use it.

God stating, that he wished for us to be rich and prosper was making no reference to worldly or material things in any way, shape, or form. Nothing in the Bible does. Worldly prosperity-speaking preachers, are preaching for the Antichrist, not Jesus Christ, you can bet your life on it. You probably already have, read your Bible. It will not mislead you, America was built on it, from day one. It has been our strength and guide since the puritans came here from England. It enabled us to whip the most powerful country on the face of the earth to obtain the freedom to worship as we pleased.

What happened to it? We have given it to Satan before we were half grown. Now Satan's people have that freedom and will not allow Christians to worship anybody but him. I wish the Christians could see how dumb that makes them look, to allow such, and act like we like it. God has said he will not always strive with man. We are about to see, he means it.

The whole story of all mankind is told in the Bible, from the beginning to the very end. Some of it thousands of years ago, not one mistake has been found in it. One of the most astonishing things I have heard of. And we still don't get it?

Religion, is a word for naming a set of laws and regulations, to bring a person or congregation of people into one body of unity. There is only one True religion, it is Jesus Christ, the Son of the Living God, the creator, for short; the *Bible*. I do not have it in me to apologize to any other religion, it is just a false religion, that is all. I cannot do one thing about that. Critics, love to say things like, religion caused the first murder on the earth, and is the cause of ever war that was ever fought.

They need to study their history a little bit. It was not true religion that caused the wars, but false religion that despised true religion. Such greed as, only two boys in the whole world and they could not get along well enough to not kill one of them. Not enough room

I guess God built the earth too small. God had already warned Cain what was going to happen. And he told him why. God wrote to us later, that where envy and strife is, there is ever evil work. If Adam and Eve would have been modern people, they would have one killed the other for sure.

Take the case of Cain and Able, that was no more or less, than premeditated murder over jealousy and envy. God did not allow them to take any vengeance upon Cain, but cast him out from among God's people, gave him the rest of the world to live in. He would be a cast out forever. It has been that way ever since, as long, as they stay away from interfering among God's people. If they cannot control one, or he don't want to be put out from among them, let the congregation have him even to putting him to death if they see fit.

If the congregation would have started out obeying God from the beginning, it would be God's people completely in charge now instead of Satan's people. And God could have been blessing them every day. Jesus would not have had to die for us. God has warned his people every day, but they would not turn their heads, nor would they raise their children in the *fear and admonition of the Lord.*

According to the heathen, God is to blame for everything. I guess that could have *some* credibility, he did make everything that was made, and put man in charge. He repented of that and is going to fix every bit of it. He turned this earth over to mankind in a perfect condition, and man gave it away, and is destroying it.

And now is blaming God for everything. I guess that makes sense to man. I do not believe God is going to be very agreeable with man on that one.

Religion, maybe the most powerful thing among mankind on the earth. Every man has his own. Has been much that way since the creation when God gave man the garden with food hanging off every tree. I have written much on how God has made most everything in twos, religion is no different. There is the true religion which is Christ the Truth. And there is the Antichrist religion which consist of every false religion on the earth and is a lie from the ground up to its crown, you can depend on it.

Look around you, if any religion does not claim the whole Word of God and in the way, it says too, then it is a false religion. God said to not let them bring it into your house. Any false religion will tell a Christian that our God says we must love everything and everybody. You can tell them for me, they are a liar, they do not know how to read the Bible like it says to read it. Why I say I do not need a deceived Christian preaching my Bible to me. Things that Satan has told him.

The carnal and the spiritual have been battling each other from the beginning and will be battling each other every day until the end. The Bible has recorded it from the beginning to the last day that time and man will exist. Man cannot clean the world up, he has too much of the world in himself. He cannot clean himself up. We can read all about it in the Bible, even before much of it has happened. It seems kind of amazing to me, there is not a false statement in it and there is not a word left out of it, and how much smarter one becomes when he starts to believe the Bible. Even though, we will not fully understand it without help from the Spirit of God, the Bible says to seek out a man of the Spirit. Or study and seek God enough and maybe you will become that help for others. I would recommend both.

I have written in all my books how anything is what it is, depending on where you are looking at it from. That is not a trick statement, it just means anyone must look at it from God's point of view, the only <u>real</u> thing. The Spirit and the carnal are looking at things from opposite sides and see very few alike. The Spirit of God is always seeing things correctly and should be in everybody while bringing them all together into one, for the betterment of the world. Why we must see things from the spiritual side to see the real thing. Carnal is just a reflection of the real thing. Among the first things one should learn is the difference between the two. If we do not know the difference between the two, how do we know which one we are in? All spirits are not of God, Satan is a copier, and very skillful at distorting the pictures with a mirror.

Together, we can pull a big load easier. Pulling against one another we can move nothing. There is a lot more people of the world than there is in the congregation of God. We can never out-pull them without help from the Spirit of God. It would be a glorious sight if we could all see and hear everything in Truth, which is Jesus Christ. Anything contrary to him is a lie and will never make it into the Kingdom of God. This can only be done in and by the Spirit of God. Our spirit must subject itself to and under the Spirit of God. It is fair and full of mercy, but stern, and has no variations in it. God will never be changed or bent around.

Mankind is so selfish and carnal he cannot fit with another man completely, only in the Spirit. This leaves out all mankind if his flesh cannot die out, how many men do you know that is agreeable to that? Religion, is simply what a person believes in and what he looks towards to put his trust into for eternity, it might not be so important if it was not so permanent, like forever. But it is the most permanent thing you will face in your entire life. God does not change.

We go through life making choices and every choice we make we will live and die with. God says we will give account for ever idle word. This does not necessarily mean we will be judged for every word we utter, but we will live for the rest of our lives, with accountability of every word after we have spoken it, without repentance. This is the reason we must be going through life repenting for we would never make it otherwise. Repenting comes from the heart, God looks nowhere else for it. He knows the thoughts and intents of all our hearts.

Can you explain that to a carnal mind? We serve God by faith, faith is believing. If we are wrong, or have done a wrong, God requires us to confess and repent.

Boy, do we hate that! Carnal minds cannot believe Truth, so it cannot have it.

Everything is at least in twos. Most things of God are in threes, that is a convincing number with God. If both sides have three witnesses, (which I have never seen) then a jury must decide which side is more convincing. God laid that out in his word. God's way of living is not difficult, just takes some common sense, the one thing we have completely taught, out of this generation and across the world. Satan, oversees this world. This is the cause of our world's condition. Satan is a lie and the father of lies. Did not God call him the god of this world? It will not improve without Truth, which is Jesus Christ. I would suggest that anybody read that line again, it is loaded.

Truth is common sense, the Bible is common sense, the only thing that will set anyone free. Freedom, is being separated from untruth, a reprobate mind loves a lie and can never be free. Taking the "Mark of the Beast" is a spiritual seal of excepting that, *never be free*, condition.

Any man that has his mind replaced with a man-made computer can never be saved without denying his flesh and moving into God's Spirit. Which is the way God has made for man to do, since Jesus was crucified. But he must believe God's Word either way, and that includes the flesh must die.

Only before we take the "Mark of the Beast" we can accept the spiritual death of Jesus Christ and go on in the Spirit of God, until our flesh decides to die carnally.

If we accept Christ now, we must live and walk in him. It is a much easier way, only we must be dead to the world. That is hard for the carnal flesh to do. Carnal flesh loves a carnal world and all the things of a carnal world including the lies. The Bible says we cannot do that and live for God. God must come before the world in our lives, your choice. He will come only with no part of a lie in him. God will not contend with our flesh and will never agree with the world. He has no use for it, we will not either after we have done away with this flesh and become all Spiritual.

It is easy to tell the difference, if one is living in the carnal world, he will be so uncomfortable, confused and bitter at life itself, which is the Spirit of God. With Satan telling him constantly, "that it is God's fault, he will not let man do what he wants to do, take what he wants to take, so he cannot be happy." Which is just another one of Satan's lies. God does not care what you do long as one does not bother someone else's same freedom. God says you treat the next man like you want him to treat you. God has given each of us our own free will, but we cannot bother one of his people that is obeying him, and not going against God's Word. God will not let him be tested beyond what he can stand. If he will stay with God, he will be delivered in a short while and God will avenge speedily. I have stood by and watched a many situation and seen God even-things up for his people, if one will just keep the faith and commune with God. But people that don't keep the faith and is not obeying God's laws, will grow into hating the truth and righteousness and anybody that lives in it. Blaming it all on God until he grows bitter toward anybody that is walking in the Spirit of God.

Study your Bible and seek God, you should be able to see for yourself everything I just wrote. If not take it to your pastor, he should be able to help you. Just keep in mind you are dealing with two worlds that do not mix. You must know which one you are dealing from, and which one you are dealing with. God will not make deals with your flesh, unless it is within his word, why we are instructed to read and live by his Word. God will give us nothing else. Whether we believe him, or trust him, or anything else, he will react within his word and one can depend on it. Our lives depend upon the Word of God, it is Jesus Christ.

6

IDENTIFYING "THE MARK OF THE BEAST"

I HAVE SAID HOW THE mark is not a carnal mark to be seen with the carnal eye but a mark inside the body, or spiritual in other words. Spiritual can only be plainly understood by the Spirit. It is a condition of a man. And can only be plainly understood by some one that is familiar with the spiritual things of man.

If you know the spirit of anything you can very well, see and know, about the life in it. Spirit is the life in anything living. And will stay very close to its source, or maybe one can say, its purpose. All spirits are not of God. A computer is *man's hope* of placing life in anything. Man has accomplished many unbelievable things, and now saying they have about perfected a computerized man, it seems nothing will surprise anyone anymore. I am sure they can fool mankind, they have already done that many times, but I would say they will never fool God, or the Spirit of God, in any way. That is not to say they will never build a computerized man. But God will never be replaced by a computer and will confidently stay in control of everything. He is *The Spirit*.

It is almost like God is playing with man to see how far he will go. But he has made his arm bare to all of us and has told us all things. Still man has not even scratched the surface of what God knows. Man has not even put a scratch on what Satan knows if he has not studied the Bible. God's Word has revealed it in the Spirit. Satan is very limited in what he can do. If God had not drawn red lines in what Satan can and cannot do, he would chew mankind up and spit him out like a plug of tobaccer.

Man is no match for a spirit without Christ to help him. Satan was defeated at the cross and is not permitted to lay one finger on anybody. But allowed to temp your mind with your own lust. And very few can stand up against their own foolish lust and selfish desires that is commonly known as the flesh. Without Jesus, God will not deal with carnal, for it is the area where man has fell from God. Man cannot font it in God's face and expect to have any communication with God, he does not sink to that level. Humility is the first step toward God through Jesus Christ, he is the mediator between God and man.

Several years ago, I communed with a kid trying to get started preaching, he had big ambitions and was explaining them to me. Saying he was trying to find a way to go straight to God the Father. I ask him if he was intending to bypass Christ? He replied, yes just him and the Father, from point A to point B, nothing in between. He had been to a little Preaching college, and some seminars, (that is educational talk, I ain't got none). I explained to him if he ever made it there he would be the most consumed person he ever heard of. No flesh will ever stand before God's presence in his glory, he will be consumed instantly is what God says. This is the reason Jesus became flesh and died for us, was to become the mediator for us to God. God had to appear to Moses covered with a very heavy black cloud. They could not look upon Moses for the brightness in his face from looking upon the trail left behind God while he was upon the mountain with him.

We are not even going to be able to blame Satan for our failures, and low estate. God knows better than that. This is the reason God will not hold Satan accountable for one thing we have done, his access to man is very limited. That saying that man came up with, "Oh, the Devil made me do it" will not hold corn shucks with God. Each man will stand in judgement for only what he has done, nobody else. God has said we are excuseless, Oman.

Man has chosen to spend eternity with evil spirits and no protection from God for we have blamed all our failures on God. And have chosen to serve Satan and all his lying carnal promises for our reward. Our flesh is going back to the dust where it came from, but our spirit and soul will live on someplace. And we think we have really showed God which way is up. When we take the "Mark of the Beast" this is what we are agreeing to, locked into the condition of a man or beast. That is really, not very smart and is fatal. I guess that is why Jesus said, in the carnal, we are blind, deaf, backwards and dead to all Truth, and foolishly hopeless. Jesus is Truth and gave himself for us. What more can he do if we refuse him?

When they were nailing him to the cross, beating and whipping him with the cat of nine tails platted with steal and bone pieces, banging the six-inch thorns into his head, pulling out his beard, spitting in his face, he prayed Father forgive them they know not what they are doing. Do you think he was lying? No, and they will never know as long, as they refuse the new birth into the Spirit. And choose to keep living in this carnal way of life, apart from God, and refusing to know him. The next time Satan gets them together and, in the mind, to kill Christ again, Jesus is going to kill all of mankind at the great battle of God Almighty, called the battle of Armageddon. And will throw *Satan*, the *Antichrist*, the *False Prophet (the Pope)* and every *soul* whose name is not written in the Lamb's Book of Life, into the lake of fire that burns forever and ever.

God said a nation that has the Lord for its God, will prosper, they will be blessed when they go out, blessed when they come in. They will not have to borrow but will have money to loan other nations. But a nation that does not have the Lord for their God will be poor, live in poverty, and owe other nations, and will perish from having the diseases and plagues that God will put on them that they feared from Egypt. The list is about fifty-three verses long in the twenty-eighth chapter of Deuteronomy, alone. It will be the last effort of God to plead with man to surrender to God, by pouring out his wrath upon the world from the spiritual side of life. During the last week (Seven-year week) left in time as we know time. Told about to the Jews there in Daniel, and to everybody, in Revelations. But his wrath is referred to, all through the Bible, that it is coming.

The way he has blessed, built, and prospered this country, I do not see how we can claim we don't know him. When the president we elected twice, outlawed our God and Bible, stood in front of the world and said, against our Supreme Court's twice ruling, this is not a Christian Nation anymore, adding to it, this is a Muslim nation, and much more.

I noticed we went down in money, under that president, double what we had ever owed from every president we ever had before him. To a figure so large one can hardly wrap one's mind around it. Are you going to tell me the people who voted for him did not notice that? Jesus said, they were blind, so I guess they did not see it. But to call them Christians, I wonder.

The Christians of today, if there are any left in this country, I do not see them. The ones that crucified Christ claimed to have done it for God. For sure, they did, but did not know that, for they did not know God. This country today is worse off than the Pharisees that crucified Jesus Christ. They did not know God either and are just as determined on annihilating all Christians as the Jews were to annihilate Jesus Christ.

Democrats, over half of this country, have been bent on impeaching Trump since God put him in office. I told them when he was elected that God put him in office, not the voters. God says he puts or rulers in office that we get. I for one, do not want to call him a liar, but over half of our country don't seem to mind at all doing just that. With a determined _intent,_ they have told every lie and used every dirty trick they know to impeach him, since he took office. When a democrat gets caught red handed, they start hollering, oh! you cannot prove intent, you must prove intent to have any case.

I would worry about my soul if I was so far from God that I could not see that Trump was a man sent from God. Obama was also sent from God but for a completely different reason, he was sent to wake God's people up. Trump was sent to allow us to save this country and will if we will not let the Democrat Liberals keep him from it. God gives us leaders from a combination of, what we want and what we deserve. He said so.

The God haters has formed a wall against him of Satan's imps that is about unbelievable and many of them calling themselves Christians, God says different. Now they have come up with a charge of obstructing justice, over a remark Trump made in a private conversation, and they can't come up with enough talk on how serious a charge it is. They have every TV station full day and night preaching on it, even to say he has single handedly wrecked our country. They are so blind they cannot see it was beat down under the Democrats until it could hardly drag itself around is why Trump was elected. Most of them will have it forgotten and believing all them lies the Democrats are feeding them before the next election.

I've been listening at them for days and have never heard the word *intent* spoken of but impeach is coming up in about every other sentence. When a Democrat is caught red handed they start hollering there is no proof of intent. They would not mention the word impeach, they called it the "I" word. And if you cannot prove intent, you have no case. I believe the shoe of intent is on the other foot this time and has been all along. But blind Christians cannot see it. It does not look like conservatives have any lawyers, they could not make a living I guess. All the money seems to be on the other side. Powerful lawyers will not move without money.

The liberal's hate toward the Lord Jesus Christ and lust toward the world and money, is about the only thing involved here, but this country's Christians cannot see that either. I keep telling myself, I must be the one who is blind, for I cannot see the Christians. Are they ashamed of it or just scared to admit it? I do not believe that is the way Christ has described his Christians. I read in Revelations where the fearful and greedy, will be locked out with the dogs and abominable, and liars.

I do not believe the illegals is the only ones that Trump needs to export from this country. With every single illegal, we should deport a Federal Judge and a Holly Wood Star and a college schoolteacher to keep them company. And maybe a bus load of left headed news reporters, just so they can have enough chummy company to party with, and every congress person they can catch. They have _intent to ruin_ this country running out both ears. I do not see how this country can operate much longer if we don't do something drastic about it. That is about the best way I can lay it out, get somebody to run it, that has the country and middle people in mind, instead of money, power, glory and authority for a lifetime for themselves.

Can you name how much gall it takes to have voted for Clintons and Obama and calling Trump a liar? You might ask Bill O'Reilly that question, only he is not close around anymore. It is below what I can imagine, like maybe the bottom of the swamp-jug. Or a speech from an established congressman, from either side, I do not see much difference.

If the left headed Devil possessed Democrats can do away with the Bible, this country is doomed to hell, and they know it. It is just that simple. The "Mark of the Beast" is just the oath they will take. Thanks to; Holly Wood, Chicago, New York, California, and Mystery Babylon there at Rome that is in-charge of our schools, and about everything else in this country that has an office phone. One lasso could about round up the six seats of Satan himself, and his playpens.

When you read over that list of names in that last paragraph, keep in mind they are the ones that are reaching for, and trying to embrace, the Antichrist Muslims' ten kingdoms that are rising in the Middle East now, to take over the world, Mystery Babylon. They will make it there for a short stance, then Christ will take over with an everlasting Kingdom of God's government with Christ and his saints and martyrs in charge. After he has used the Antichrist kingdoms to burn Mystery Babylon's city off the earth there at Rome, with its hypocrites. He will warn his people to come out of her before he does it, but they had better hear him.

These are the wars that Christ was talking about and will be this that is now starting to take place. Fulfilling the Bible prophecy that is at hand now, starting up with a slow start, but moving faster and faster as it gets here. God has said for us to get prepared. Knowing him is about all the preparation we can make, or maybe building a bomb shelter, the more the better. He has promised to lead his people through.

We must believe him, for believing is faith, and faith is the only thing God will honor. If we know God we will trust him, so we must know him. Jesus has made a way to live in each of our hearts. If we will just open the door and receive him. The process and condition are called, "born again." The people that think born-once is enough, as one person told me her

Church taught, has just denied the Spirit of God. And he is a Spirit. When they die, who is going to resurrect them? I would be afraid to deny the Spirit, that would be the same thing as denying God. Jesus gave his carnal body for a sacrifice and went completely back into the spirit and sent their Spirit back to live in the ones that will receive it. I do not put much hope in anything else.

The Spirit is life to anything that has life in it. Nobody but God has the control over his Spirit. He will not force anyone to receive him but will give everybody a chance. Carnal, man gets everything backwards to God, I just heard some preaching lately and you would think they were preaching that the Spirit needed to join carnal man to survive. But I don't think they knew how it was sounding to mankind. Of course, that was sounding much better to men that are lost. They are looking for a preacher that will blame it on God and make them look as good as everybody else. But the Spirit of God is not the one that needs born again and become a new creature.

Every man will receive a just reward for all his works. God is a fair judge, and will reward every man for all his Works, and God is the only thing that can save man. His Word has already judged everything. Carnal just cannot comprehend such a thing. When you are reading the Bible, you are reading God's judgment on everything that is hearing it. One cannot understand that without help from the Spirit of God, and you must believe it by faith.

To them that doubt the Bible, read where Daniel describes the countries of England, Russia, and the country of America. He did it four thousand years ago. And describes the Antichrist Kingdoms of ten kings coming up later, that rules and destroys the Mystery Babylon Kingdom that grew so long, big, and powerful there at Rome. And tried to rule the world through religion for so many years. America defeated them in two world wars, but Satan has worn out the saints like God said he would. Daniel wrote his writings maybe, four thousand years ago. He was a very smart man to describe the countries four thousand years before they existed. I believe he had the Spirit long before it was given to all men.

John the revelator, the disciple that Jesus loved, did his writings two thousand years ago at the start of Mystery Babylon and told us about her that is two thousand years old now. John told us about the beginning and end of her, two thousand years ago, and not one word has been off mark this far. He also told us the end times until God himself comes down from heaven and makes his abode among men after the creation has been burned up. The end is just about in sight now just like he told it. I have never read where we are going to heaven, but where God is bringing heaven down to us.

All the prophets of the Bible establish each other's writings anywhere in it. How anybody who can read and watch the news today and not see that the Bible is authentic I can never understand. It is no wonder that

Jesus said, Satan has blinded their minds, the light of the glorious gospel cannot shine into their hearts and they cannot be saved. When one is Spiritually dead, they are dead, period. There is no other way to say it. The carnal is dead and does not know it.

How many men over a hundred years old do you see around you, not many for sure, and it would be a safe bet them you do see do not have long left. By strength and for sure, clean positive living, they are living thirty years over their allotted time.

I remember when I was a small boy, well over seventy years ago, most of the Spirit filled churches believed that the book of Revelations was a spiritually written book, and could not be understood by ordinary men, and it was very much left alone. But now about any person that labors in the word can explain at least some about any place in Revelations. I understand why now, mankind was not matured enough to receive and handle the understanding well and was being confused trying too. It is still a confusing book to anyone that gets ahead of God in any place in it or will not establish every word as God said to do. This, is why God said for us to establish every Word of God with, at least, two are three witnesses.

This must mean, from the Word of God, for God does not receive the word-of-man for a witness, Jesus says so. If man could receive this law, it would narrow every denomination down to one. I'd say that would be a powerful scripture, enough for me to embrace for quite a while. Which I intend to do.

Where man has a problem of believing God and keeping the faith, it is hard for man to fully realize this world and the Spirit of God's world is fully two different worlds. The world cannot talk the language of the Spirit of God; the Spirit of God cannot talk the language of man on man's level. Flesh would be consumed just to be in the presents of the Holy God's Glory. Jesus must connect the two worlds in communication. It is not because God *thinks* he is too holy for us, it is because he *is too* holy for us. That should let us have an Idea of how much of an improvement it is to be reborn into the Glories of God and how much we need it.

It puts a new meaning on the word Glorious. If God shared his glory with us now, it would burn up this flesh with our heart and blood, and leave just our necked soul without a body to put it in. God will not save us until we prove to him we have a soul that will be willing to come into his Spirit and be happy with it and a new spiritual body. It seems that many people are not even interested in it, because they cannot believe God. Their flesh will never become interested in it. For it is doomed, God will never accept it.

The complete Bible stays the same. The complete human race, world, and time itself; the complete spirit world, everything you can name or think of that is built and passing with time is all built like an ice cream cone, starting at a point and getting larger as it gets older. It is growing bigger as it gets taller and longer. Humanity is getting more into carnal knowledge in everything you can think of. Life is getting faster and the load is getting heavier. Time is moving faster, and more is expected of each person every day.

I do not care what the doctor's figures come up with, there are more people dying every day than there every has been in history. More diseased and disabled people than the world has ever seen before. It is going to get much worse and faster. I will try to shut down on the figures I cannot produce proof of, but I do not believe one can produce figures that will prove me wrong. But I believe I have made my point.

When is it going to run out and where is it going to? We have developed a mentality of thinking we are in control and can handle anything that jumps up, and common sense tells us we cannot do that. We cannot even keep in control of our own minds. We are getting involved heavy into the spiritual world, that is God's world and his business much more than the carnal world. We are not about to steal God's seat and throne. Though it seems like every Christian organization on the globe is trying to.

I believe he is getting tired of being ignored and pushed around. I do not picture him as getting scared or worried, but maybe tired. He has said he will not always strive with man and is going to have to put an end to us all soon. If we study the Bible, we can know the end just don't know the time but are told if we watch the signs we will know the nearness thereof. I believe it is safe to say, more than probably, no person living today will be living when the Lord comes back again. It will be a generation that we produced and inherited, a civilization that we helped to build. Left them no training to better it. For we have not bettered it either.

This carnal fleshly world is just got so long to exist, and we have even a shorter time. We will be destroyed with it, if that is our preference. If we choose to live and die with Satan, he has lived passed his opportunity, so will have we. If we do not believe and love God and his Holy Righteousness, we will not live with God, for that is all that will be with him.

With enough time and your patience, I could set down with anybody and read to you every promise that I have wrote here, from the Bible with conformation. If you have a pastor, he should be able to help you with it. God said, he that labors in the word is more blessed.

I am not saying that you need to make yourself miserable in this world, far from it. Of course, we have plainly already done that. I will say if you are happy with this world and think that is the blessings of God, I would have my doubts for you, God has said much about that. Like, we are not to love this world nor the things of this world, for the love of the Father is not in them and they will all pass away. And many other such things God has said plainly.

He did not say we should not be happy, just not happy in the things of the world. Remember I started this subject out with there are two worlds, we are to let this world freely go, get it out of our system. Many will miss heaven, because they will not agree with that and will try to hang onto this world and try to be content with it. That is just not going to happen to God's people.

If God allowed this world to flood into his world it would be no better than this one. There can be a lot of questions on that subject, about all of them would be around the judging of others department, and I have learned to leave that up to God. I cannot speak with any authority on that subject, only what God's Word says. But I will stick my neck out just a little if for no other reason, just to let people know, there is a fine line there and we all must be very careful. Here I go, Joyce Meyer has a glorious Ministry, I love her dearly, we need a lot more of her, drastically, and I do not believe I've ever heard her cross over the line, but she can sure keep me doing a lot of praying for the both of us. Her ministry is a little one-sided, not untrue but not very well balanced. Other preachers should make up the other side.

There is not much Scripture in the Bible promising me joy and security in the world affairs. Enough said, probably too much, but I hope one can see the line that I was referring too. My whole purpose, all of God's Word is wrote from the Spiritual perspective. Of course, her preaching is centered around the fact that we can be happy despite what the world throws at us. She gets that across.

Jesus died for us when we were not worthy, we must have him there at the end to claim us. We can never make ourselves worthy, just have him there with and for us at the end is enough. Might keep in mind, carnal man always thinks backwards to God, he is not here to serve us, we are here to serve him. It should be a real pleasure if we can just turn loose of this World that people and Satan has polluted until God will not have it. And is going to burn it up, with the elements thereof. But is willing to save them that can love righteousness.

We should be willing to die before receiving the "Mark of the Beast." It is at the end of the line and close to being permanent. We need to be forewarned for when it gets here, times and circumstances are going to be very different and hardly recognizable. Someone that does not know something about what is in the Bible, will not be apt to survive. And will not be expecting what they see. No one will survive without the Spirit of God. There is no other way.

The complete Bible is about staying with God even if they have a knife at your throat. Then we will have to rely upon the Scripture that he will not let more come upon us than we can bare. But we will have to be prayed up and walking close to God to have that kind of faith. I say if Daniel would have waited until they threw him into the lion's den to start up his pray line, we might be reading where Daniel was eaten up by the lions. How long did Joyce pray and seek God to get where she is at?

A LITTLE ABOUT WHAT GOD SAYS ABOUT THE RAPTURE; NOTHING:

I HAVE READ MY BIBLE about as much as the next man. I have said in all my books that I have never seen the word, rapture, in the Bible. I have seen the places where they have taken it from. One place is the fourth chapter of the Book of Revelations. John was called up in the Spirit to see what was in the hereafter. I have read what some Bible scholars has said the word hereafter meant, like it was a complicated word. They got it complicated when they tried to make it mean what they wanted it to.

The word hereafter, could be turned around into after here and mean the same thing as far as I can see, and not have any complications about it. They were talking about time and it was referring to the time of when he was talking, and after. I do not care if it is Finis Dake, I do not like for somebody to monkey around with words in my Bible. Jesus said not to, but I can give them slack, that there is a drastic change took place there at that spot, Revelations forth chapter in the Bible.

John was called from an open door in heaven instructing him to come up here. What man can tell you where heaven is at? The scientist says, something like the space above our atmosphere or solar system. The Bible does not explain where it is or how high up is. Sounds to me like when someone is trying to tell you where it is to prove his theory is looking for an argument, and one would do well to leave it alone. That could run into contention quickly, God has said to leave that alone.

I see nothing there to start a rapture with. I had one preacher say, "Well, it did say we would be called up into the air." If heaven is in the air it is not above the atmosphere, make up your mind. I believe it might be better explained to admit the carnal cannot see a Spirit or anything that is in a spirit with carnal eyes unless it shows one an image of the thing.

Well, enough of the shaky junk that I've wrote to make a small point, people who try to build a word to put in the Bible that is not there, has a problem. The Bible says to establish every word with two or three witnesses before it can be accepted as a gospel word. It would be required to come from the Word of God for Jesus said he will not accept the witness of man, for he knows what is in a man.

Another place that sounds a lot like a rapture to me is in the twenty-fourth chapter of the book of Mathew where Jesus says, at the sound of a trumpet he will gather together all his elect from the four winds of heaven. Reading other places for conformation, I am convinced that he is referring to his gathering them to him there at Armageddon in the hills around Jerusalem, where him and his disciples and Israel are at and will be ruling the world with an iron hand during the millennial reign. If you find the establishing Scripture it will be resurrected Saints and martyrs, ruling on earth from Armageddon. This will tie in with the starting in of the fourth chapter of the book of Revelations, where everybody seems to recognize that there is a big change that takes place there. It is why they try to build the rapture in that space, they do not know what happened there. I have not seen anybody that can make a rapture like they preach fit there and not contradict a bundle of Scriptures in other places. Everything from the forth chapter on out is spiritually written seen from in heaven. I see not one scripture that will establish a rapture there or anywhere else, while God has told us to establish every Word of God with at least two or three other places in the Bible. As to the meaning of every Word and how it is used.

I have put the word, _establish_, in every book I have wrote, and tried to explain the meaning and of how it is used, I fully believe it could eliminate all Denominations but one if properly used, if people would understand and use it like the Bible says. I have not heard the word being preached, though it is a Bible, word. After the thousand-year perfect reign of Jesus, and Satan being locked up with a seal on him, the Antichrist and the False Prophet been thrown into hell already. The earth will receive a great reviving of population with the peaceful, prosperous, rule, of the Jews and Jesus Christ. Remember all them things Jesus said about the gentiles being put under the Jews? Read about it there.

This will cover time for many of Jesus' remarks he has said he will do on this earth. Starting at the fourth chapter of Revelations, the earth and mankind will be operating under complete different times in the Bible, but God himself has not changed. People of today will probably not be living in that time but we should be studying our Bibles and living toward them times, and most of all teaching our kids about what God is going to do. This is what is wrong in the world today, no kids I know about has been taught or raised in the fear and admonition of the Lord and his Word.

You know that some people will be teaching that Christ has delayed his coming and will turn to living for themselves. Christ has not delayed his coming, it just has a lot to happen before he comes, and we have been preaching hard that he is going to rapture us any day, which is a lie. One may be called out to meet him any day, they are burying many people every day. There is going to be many wars and much killings and sufferings, times like no man has ever seen and will never see again. Because the people are working farther from God in every way, every day. The world is going to be killed down to a scary few people before God intervenes with his millennial reign and saving of the Jews, his people.

After the millennial reign Satan will be released to gather the kings and princes of every nation of the world to come against Jesus for the last battle of the Lord, also called the battle of the great day of God Almighty, there at Armageddon. This will be the final weeding out of all mankind. May also be the shortest war on record, I would not know, but Jesus will handle it. Best I can see, it may be the first and last time for Jesus and Lucifer to meet face to face in a battle. It will be a short one, looks like Jesus will have a complete clean-up day. Satan will have the biggest army ever formed on the earth.

God sent him to gather the complete and final number of what belong to him. Jesus will roll the whole thing into the Lake of Fire that burns forever and ever, along with every soul whose name is not written down in the Lamb's Book of Life. It will bring about the end of Christ's thousand-year reign on the earth and that will bring about the end of time as we know time in this creation.

Read about it in chapters: sixteen and seventeen of the book of Revelations. The change at the forth chapter in Rev. is a Spiritual change, from there on out is just completely Spiritual. I could not find where any carnal thing played one part in it or had anything to say in it. At the start of the fourth chapter, John was called up to heaven to see what was in the hereafter, everything he look at was from and by the Spirit of God.

When I was a kid the reason people did not read much in the book of revelations, they thought it was only spiritually written and understood. But as we thought we were getting more mature God has been reviling it to us more and more. But a lot of people getting ahead of God get a lot of things wrong about what it says. When two people cannot get their scriptures to agree, one of them is wrong, and easily both can be wrong. Somebody is not *establishing* their scriptures as the Bible says to do.

Anybody that thinks he can just establish the Bible as he sees it, is wrong, the Bible teaches it will establish itself if you can use it right. Run the word establish down in your Bible. It says to establish every word with at least two and three witnesses. I have never found where the Bible establishes the same word two different ways. That is why I do not allow anybody to monkey with a word in my King James Bible, Jesus said, to not change one word in it. I am not particularly fond of hearing it preached wrong. Every man will have to answer for himself, but I found nothing about carnal anywhere in the book after the start of the fourth chapter. It is not written like or in the same matter as the rest of the Bible. I have written in all the rest of my books that everything is what it is, according to where you are looking at it from. This is a good example of what I was talking about. The Book of Revelations, after the fourth chapter, was obviously written looking from Heaven. I have been years in figuring out what was so different about it. The difference was obvious but for years I could not explain it.

I do not believe one ever comes to the place where he knows it all. God says when one thinks he has become wise, he becomes foolish. I would say, we are not very good at evaluating ourselves, for whatever it is worth.

I see one big problem with this whole world of mankind, nobody seems to know who is at the top, and in charge. Why God says it is required for a man to know *him* to be accepted by *him*. It is very natural for any man to want to be in total charge of himself and resents anybody having charge over him. That leaves every man in charge of himself.

When we know no two men can be in total agreement on few, if anything, and there is not a fair overseer, that knows everything, trusted by everybody, to work things out, you will have a chaos situation. Like the world is in now. Do you know any such body? That overseer, can only be God Almighty, the creator of everything in or about our creation. Anyone that cannot see and accept them truths, will not be taken into God's new creation. Seems to me anyone can see that if he will humble himself, come off his High Horse and fit into this creation God has given us. Everything must be established by the Word of God.

It is for sure not one of us mortal men can handle the job. Jesus could not do it and I do not think you or me can either. Reckon that was not what God is talking about all along? Humble oneself, is the first requirement that is required by God, to be accepted into God's kingdom. I did not plan it that way but seems like all my books are turning into evangelizing books, I believe that is all right, I am sure it is God's doing. I have been determined to make every word to be stabilizable by the Word of God.

Someone told me once, that nobody finishes a book, you must set a date and stop writing. I am starting to believe him. It's been a blessing to me. I hope it can be a blessing to somebody else.

I have written something in this book about everything from Adam and Eve in the garden, to the birth and crucifixion of Jesus Christ. Him sending back his "Spirit at Pentecost," to the "Mark of the Beast" and Christ throwing the Devil, the Beast, and the False Prophet into the Lake of Fire. Where they shall be tormented day and night for ever. I have tried to write it like I am telling you the story, I have left very little off the table. I hope nothing is left unexplained. BGW

Printed in the United States
By Bookmasters